Half a Pint of Tristram Shandy

Jo Pearson
Daithidh MacEochaidh
Peter Knaggs

route

First Published in 2001 by Route
School Lane, Glasshoughton, West Yorks, WF10 4QH
e-mail: books@route-online.com

ISBN: 1 901927 15 6

Cover Design: Jackie Parsons

Support::
Ian Daley, Isabel Daley Galan, James Gilligan, Judith Payne

Printed by Cox and Wyman, Reading

A catalogue for this book is available from the British Library

Events and characters in this book are imaginary.
Similarity to real persons and events is coincidental.

Full details of the Route programme of books
and live events can be found on our website
www.route-online.com

Route is the fiction imprint of YAC, a registered charity No 1007443

Half a Pint of Tristam Shandy was created as part of The Opening Line, a
writer development project run by Yorkshire Art Circus in partnership
with the Word Hoard. The Opening Line was funded by the National
Lottery through the Arts for Everyone scheme.

YAC is supported by
Yorkshire Arts, Wakefield MDC, West Yorkshire Grants

Talking To The Virgin Mary
Jo Pearson

Contents

Part One: Pit Spots

Gala

Thirty five years to the day
they set off down that dual carriageway
to play bingo at Scarborough
the place they met and honeymooned.

Half way the exhaust pipe
slipped off like lost love
their marriage collapsing
and bouncing down the hard shoulder

Coral ecstatic to her two wins
him a full house of losses.

Size

She is hole, a cheap shoe
in which he fits his sticky big toe
at his drunken leisure
no sweaty socks poking in too tight
he don't care if it rubs
so long he get his pussy graze

then walks away
her left bereft
a worn out shoe an empty hole
depressed now everyone knows
she's an easy loafer
a shoe stepped in shit by accident.

Someone's New Home

In memory of Brian.

There'd been no rubbish
no weekly stack of decadence
for the bin man, day glo peach
curtains closed for months.

Overnight, autumn came
down on the black sacks
piling by his door

as though he'd been collecting
the trash of himself
holding it back
till death could smack it
against the council wall

still waiting for the refuse men.

Smile for Derek

Thumbprinted on my creased up corners
get me out when you're on your own
or with your buds after fifteen pints.

You can find me somewhere at the top
down a side aisle
WH Smiths brown paper bag
could say I'm serviceable
help you keep it going with the wife.

You stash me with the others
underneath the bed not hers his side
paper chain lovers
could wall paper a whole room
with their wishful thinking bile.

Shooting Star

Queenie died now she's a satellite
looking down on him
selling her pride the television
for a few grams
of inherited temazepam.

Feeding on her
part baked sympathy cake
drinking Tennants extra cheap
a Christmas spent awaiting payment
feigning grievance, getting dried

we tried she said
and went home tired.

Trichology

It started when she were eleven
these hairs appearing from every pore
they shaved her in the hospital
stealing to buy depilatory cream
slapping it on
that's what it's like to be a woman.

Her so drawn
an albino hedgehog frightened to shift
from some cramped hotel dorm
a new dawn when the greys come.

Getting her moustache electrocuted
and having to pay the skinny fur ball
her boyfriend calls
sideburns, arm pits, naval as new
pulling her hair out.

Crash

She is windscreen
air freshener around her neck
Mica in the mirror
wakes to her new features
make an impact.

Eyes brighten
distorted smile
a pink smudge of lipstick paste
she is weeping violins.

Do You Believe in Betty Blue?

Star constellation freckles Zorg
selling the piano
cutting her hair off
so no other man look
zipping her lips up
cracking her hips apart.

Star constellation freckles Zorg
gouges out
a disapproving fuck
her big bear
that obsidian orion
ploughs fists of insults.

Prime Time

Silent one of her mother's fragrant farts
overcome before she realises
purgatory in motion
picking dry sick stains on a tatty nightdress.

Do some healing
bizarre yoga practice circa 1977
Lyn Marshall and her slick positions

accusing her that bottle of junior aspirin
without a label from the mantlepiece
said she took too much on board

then like a yo-yo hesitant to leave
one Steve Reich track on the cd
stinking air puckered with spud guns.

Still Born

I can see him.
From deep within
the eye of my breast
I see him.

His gaze bores a hole
through the middle
of my forehead.

My baby
pressed against my chest,
growing cold, born dead.

I cry tears like petals,
petal tears of blood red
dripping on his face.

Fatalism

Morbid,
she grew up with a fascinating death wish.

Fatalistic,
she'd walk home lonely
late at night,
listen to The Smiths
and smoke
because she was hoping for an early death.

Later,
life took over
her rubble body
as blood erupted from her
in a bleak cascade
and ended
her deal with melancholy.

Do it Anyway

Feel the fear and hide away for sixteen years
breathe outside air through a crack
in a council flat pane of glass
light a cigarette with a safety match
bribe someone else to post the mail
don't hang up that tv aerial
the duvet cover's pepper red
lay side by side aside the contraception, pet
nobody nag that it stalled in its tracks
this love lost on an outside bet.

Goddamn Lucky Girl

They walk the street
that haunts her brave companion.
The death of his son by certain means
dare not ask the house number.

He wants his children
to relinquish those ties
dissolve into her coffee eyes
these thistles in his kiss of life.
In her dilemma she gives him her safety harness
and cocooned in his love envelope
treads the high wire.

They embrace on the balustrade
stand in rain
spill pills like melted smarties.

Another Night In

Pregnant with pain
his Pochohontos
comes to her now
with a flake that he bought.

In a clothes menagerie
salt and pepper shaken
catch a liquorice kiss
from his sticky bud tongue.

Toast a heal of bread
drinks from his coffee bucket
colours become keener
the more that is smoked.

Her lycra leggings
of brightest yellow
always wrangling for love.

Part Two: Side Section the Coal Face

Spaced, 1999

For Chris

The first big weekend of the summer was filled
by the mystery disappearance of the big Strappelli:
this new age hippy policeman Noah
predicted floods midsummer's day the year 2000
suffered headaches and sinusitis prior to thunder
stuck a cushion on his head for balance
began to make elaborate plans to build his own F14 bomber
still in Blue Peter paper nose dive stage.

The speculation of him being in a tractor
somewhere in East Anglia continued the debacle
they had to bin his cooked kitchen pans.
A woman phoned twice at half eleven
threatening coppers when he's twenty seven
but they really don't know where he is.
Leonard only left him to bob out to the bookies.

The penny dropped two days to realise
the failed Russian chess champion
had taken his belongings
one pouch of baccy and a photo of him
holding his jobseeker's allowance
taken on her camera from the mantlepiece
they don't know how they didn't notice

some dreadful premonition he had
about Nostradamus and the date July 20th
responsibility of nothing doing on the telly
making him restless like Reggie Perrin
an anonymous trip to the South of France
to start something big.

Con Man

Monsieur Celibate is a back tracking needle
no monk on retreat
that'd take more than a vasectomy.
We'd broadcast his number
but it would rip a seam
walking into DX Communications
on Groundhog day.

She wants to bell Davy
right away to tell him the news
that the pressure of one huge Devil's claw chain
is off with his bonsai aphrodite.

And what colour's yours
have you not got one yet
sat in the penguin café like scrambled eggs
welded together badly the 1970's
chromium toilet roll holder with added ashtray.

There's an old aroma in the living room
cooking up new ingredient lies
with soap white fibre optic hair
a pregnant smile and ocean eyes.

Some public school boys
can't put down their bat and balls
admit pet lipped they let slip
the wrong code.

Talking to the Virgin Mary

Last night she talked with Jesus
he came in with a single tin of Heineken export
making crumbs of ash on the carpet
gifts of fleas said listen babe
I know I'm delusional
but should I get my bronze curly mass
of hair cut off or leave it natural
what's the best way to score a girlfriend?

She sneezed across the room
you can't cuddle up to a poem
that semi- domestic burning the single bed
said it was the loudest he'd heard her in years.

But it's hard out wearing an emergency poncho
my premature beer belly buying cheap baccy
I read the bible every day
eighteen months not in hospital
working with my hands I'm doing ok.

Last night she talked with Jesus
said he's having problems keeping friends
she stays indoors eyes averted
like Stan and Hilda to a painted mural
on her drab room wall some hyper space portal
living on candles, apples and stale air.

He's stopping down he says this winter
it being that time of year again.

Lengths

For Dandelion

Waiting for Dandelion's Salvation Army bra
thinking I missed her empty top pockets

come toked out steaming from Derek's
dilated eyes at a fumbled promise.

12.50 to Tom for an eigth
fat bargain at that rate.

He ordered me naked
below waist bent knees
didn't mention his weaving loom
were up in the attic
said with sad tits like envelope flaps
I'd be big in Japan
untied my shoe laces.

I'm an Icelandic sex therapist
twenty quid blow job
to the man with one arm
don't mean to be pedantic
but he patted my arse way slow
a 33rpm bed in.

Slipping a bra strap
every latent dragging footstep
that comes around the corner
combat boot style.

An Unplayed Piano Grimaces

For Rico

Teeth clattering like a twelve tone row
he passed her back the cigarette
ashtray that she is.
Sat there yellow boned
at the stagnant wedding reception lottery
sluicing rain outside.

Teeth clattering like uneven knitting
smelling an arm pit
so he can recognise her when he's blind
slicing the wedding cake atmosphere
feigning enjoyment, congratulations
strangers jaws vexed in strained smiles.

Teeth clattering like a play station instruction
face badly pritt-sticked on
the flower lady a 1995 elderberry wine
shining in a too tight dress
buffing up for pregnant hours.

Teeth clattering like a single tap shoe
the gin and tiffin taken down
friends with everyone for fifteen seconds
the party smooth as a ride
on her bike with the buckled tyre.

Teeth clattering like a warm air heater
tell her that you love her
in less than ten words on the back of a cereal pack
name that tune in thirty minutes
from a bland DJ to an empty dance floor.

Unsmiling children hang out
teeth clattering like acute nausea.

Suicide Brunette

For Al

Christmas with Lara
doesn't inspire her
soothe or motivate
elicit any lust

like sitting through
an old black and white musical
at her grandmother's
tv that time of year is even odds.

Christmas with Lara
now it's boxing day
the day after the day after
time a worn out mongrel
when she's doing so much.

Christmas with Lara
should've written it
on a piece of paper
everyone's a doctor
got some switch to pull or push.

Christmas with Lara
does it for us
stuck in some pointless occupation
on the eve of a new millennium
twisting our ankles.

Enid

For Andy and Carla

Her mother's Elvis:
superimposed dwarf with excess facial hair
and nail extensions
plays down the working men's club
third Friday night each month
to half a dozen punters.

Small breasts middle age come back
star spangled flares
take of sideburns and a rayon chest wig

has a secret double life
by day crippled from a frozen shoulder
arm in a sling
same arm poking its mental stick

by night transformation
while husband Bobby
puts the karaoke tape into the machine
and biddies about with limited spot lights.

Wouldn't think she goes to physio
three times a week
is on mobility steroid injections.

Living in America the bed end stadium size tv
Elvis is well killing his tunes in Whitby.

Piano Fingers

Come in kiss the cat
some axe murderer drove her back
flooring his station taxi -all that wrath.

Not just the taxi the phone calls stopped
suspended in time a broken transit van
knew the inevitable but not when

or the venue, day,
workshop in the YMCA
wrong moment right place
leaving for the outside getaway ride.

The lightbulb flashed, flicked, flickered,
thought about it more than once
Lavinia from Italy said the best thing
for that ailment
is Ricola from Holland and Barrett.

Riding that big belly ache tide
frivolous door won't stop chiming
body needing to supine
jaw's buckled down
things happen like doctor's rounds
and a woman phones at eight to check she's alive.

"Come in fifty seven come in fifty seven
don't tell them where you're going
you know where you're going
but don't let them know
that you know where you're going
fifty four finishing hope street
five four finishing hope street."

It's savoury, it's savoury she's after
but the new chunky Dairylea cheese triangles
dividing twine is locked inside its wrapper
left the vocal animator
in a house on southwark street
his desperate generosity
were a burnt upside down pear cake.

Pickle in kerosene, TCP, hydrogen peroxide,
Windowlene and amoxycillin until he's seen
in rainbow colours searching for his coat
pain's muted her from same tactical positions
an ill fitting rivet cross threaded and hammered home.

Snapping the sneck on a door of sanctions
sanding off more and more Henry Moore
unavailable for eyesight, work, coffee drop ins.

And as she were leaving he knew she were on one
the cat slept on his side
her heart felt a slight draught
but she's ok now cutting her finger nails to the skin.

Buspirone

She feels better now
the night has blackened
coloured in the sky
and one more day is gone

and wonders why
feeling his keen breath hot on her neck
and bronze bristles trace a breast
does not move her.

Is it in the skin peeling yellow
cigarette end hair losing dye
in long pewter shreds
the gravity of being so light?
Doesn't help to know
the sun's been eclipsing the moon
always.

Four bicycles stolen and what to do
about a bruised shin
but copper up for taxi rides
and worn out shoes
this love riddled with obstacles.

Next day leans its way
reluctantly on their lives again
pushes in the queue.

She feels calmer now
her diesel anger has been
siphoned off in screaming silence
cloistering these troubles
between him and a minimum dose.

On the Cusp of Things

For Fynn

She is liquid nutritious sipping drink
she is the amphibian that sits on top a fig leaf
a piece of flock caught dragging upstream
fitting in, being complacent, a condiment,
an after dinner tooth pick
squeezed between two fingers a resistant flea
blob of orange plasticine
different dress for each eventuality.

Has the memory of a fish
cold water, zygotic, big lips,
no place to live let alone swim
lines that maps her fins
drawn in with an indelible felt tip.

Should have been twinned
forcep separated, two hearts bleeding
one shiny pin, one mirror image
that bit of vim round the toilet rim
some soapy scum on an overdue bath
spot of froth skimming the North sea
the most bereft sign of the zodiac
when the sun is at his lowest
and the moon hides away in the trash bin.

Tudor Music

For Tudor

Last night he said meeting her
were like a fugue in a carpet
that were before losing consciousness.

Cracking joints she fingered all
the well tempered claviers and toccatas
from beyond the back of dog ears and torn corners
photostats hold up in the sideboard.

The carpet in monody
dark purple and molting
later accompanied by a royal red rug
two pound from the car boot sale
the dog ogled.

Pitched voices chant, chatter, digress
go off on a tangent, agree at last
her favourite e minor.

Then he wanted to play
her washboard chest
an altogether different kind of music.

Putting up the Relatives

Boris Yeltsin was sitting in the Strappelli chair
unzipping his overcoat
didn't give no warning
could have phoned the phone's on incoming
Russian embassy they'd pay
just went and retired while they weren't watching the news
new rules during the festive period
took a train for the journey
to see his comrades.

Felt at home
in the north facing knife edge draught
hovering round a cranked up gas fire
oven on full with nowt in it
doors pulled to
windows ever so slightly still open.

Didn't please the leader of the African National Congress
already fell down stairs loaded at Christmas
cracking on he's paralysed by gun warfare
sat in the best chair huff and puff
getting a cleaner in, lording the moment.

Strappelli just been released all this happen
now a fashion accessory
the latest slapper test
hit in the shin with a pair of crutches.

Boris were the only one saw it
the New Messiah stood up in the middle of the carpet
craning over the Christmas tree (no lights)
said they were all weird as fuck.

Apron Strings

Crazy vegetarian daughter
calls herself some kind of musician
she's crisp thin, that'll do it
a tin of Heinz all day breakfast
shoved through the cat flap
6 o'clock on Sunday morning.

And that lemon squeezer
can't be too sophisticated
to have one.
I'm up to my boots
with doing the Sharlston
that tweed hat I like's
best thing to keep me 'ead wahm.

Don't speak me, the wife, son,
daughter-in-law, workshite boyfriend
and I ant seen me brother since jubilee year
our anniversary is on the 22nd.

Show her we can this winter
have two pair of everything
hospital corners, an even suntan.

Theme and Variations

1.
When there is nothing much left
she is the stocking filler
a single satsuma shoved to the toe end.

No clementine
squashed between the tangerines
and monkey nuts

pithy satsuma

if he ever came to peel her
she'd spit in his eye.

2.
When there is nothing much left
she is soup
that tin of Campbell's
lumpy at the back of the kitchen cupboard.

Enough for two
hidden behind the packet Smash
and glace fruit

cream of mushroom

if he ever came to choose her
she'd spill down his top
up the front.

Taxi Man

She couldn't reach him by phone,
had tried twice, thought of ringing the hospital.
Joan didn't think to phone
and tell her he was in intensive care
and died
before she could say goodbye.
She loathed herself but couldn't forgive HER.

I am her protector, friend, lover.
I am the taxi man, try to please everyone,
spread myself too thin, take you anywhere.
I am Judas on the cross,
Sebastian with his arrows,
her only family, lonely and lost.

She wanders through the ether now
in a carcass body.
In fear she flies,
lives in a barren world of needles and cocktails.
Sees deformed men with ten foot cocks,
desperate to flee, running on the spot.
Sees spangles and marbles and fire crackers and angels,
stockpiles stagnant tampons
to whip out and fling like flags of defeat
on unsuspecting visitors.

Bastard Landlord

Grinding glass sex education periods as they spoke
making secret letter bombs out of used tampax
leave the front door open if friends call round
freehold for burglars
unreliable tenant in that fully furnished student flat
with sky tv, microwave oven
and downstairs shower attachment
then the aliases'd start.

Like every other lazy smoker Ellen
gangster moll scarlet lipstick smacked right on
eloped with sucked in cheek skins
at the state of rizlas to the valley of the dolls.

Now the rest are plying her to attend
musicians nights, late night barbequeues
poetry events at that address
her left playing on the nose flute
a voice enough to break a swan's neck
pretends she's given up trying
to make amends to covert ASH members.

Wasting a cheap biro testing the consistency
door to door ballot poll of relevant postal districts
sleep on the outside
torture him with the crenellation marks
of her knicker elastic
give Bob Marley back his single bed.

Fin Rot

A pink eyed bloated shabumpkin
dips for a tepid fin
that looks well smoked
resin scales resting
but starts to float

and watches the machine
wash him inside out
and watches the machine
drip blips in his gill

not filleted or breadcumbed
but battered and boil in the bag
death ready smell
kept at bay with sea salt

and on the bone fixing a rosary
sorting one small fairground bag of stuff
two unlit matches
two round rimmed frames
a coastal phrase for fishes in a bucket.

Lathered in butter sauce
asked how she were going
listing the people they knew
who'd done the same thing
and got away with it
now she's not allowed to visit

that snow storm bought for his birthday
cracked from bottom to top
him complaining of shit black as the ocean
the blood in his piss, the shit in his blood

plastering the serenity prayer aside his bed
like she said she would weeks ago
mucking out the goldfish bowl.

Dominatrix

She is a blue rose
shares his secrets, truths, phantasies, shame
discreet in letters on the page
explicit in telephone conversations
illicit kisses remain
where they see no ray.

She beckons
no mother, child bearer, comforter.
a chameleon with fingerprint impressions
rekindles forty candles
eases back the midrif pain.

She will cane, slap
tie his hands against his back
on the meun piss, shit, blood
fill his dwindling libido cup.

The georgette panties sent worn warm
in perfumed tissue tied with ribbon
hand wash in cold
dab with cologne
dry on a sunlit volvo dashboard.

She will do him anything
wet thought at the next load of laundry
he need only beg.

Trolleys Round the World

Untainted imaginations let us
take a trip in a trolley round the world.
Receptacle that once held worldly goods
no greater than your daily bread and butter
now yielded passions a plenty
like travel to far flung places by magic carpet,
like Egypt or some other Byzantine bazaar.

I was once persuaded, aged six,
to show you my other lips.
In the big playground, my deflowered
smooth upturned white triangle – with centre slit
felt the slight thrill of Autumn breeze.
(Furtive glances from side to side
for inadvertent onlookers).

You showed me you little boy's companion,
small plasticine worm squirming
between the fingers of your hand,
soft and malleable, fascinating.
(It didn't stop us that we knew
we were being naughty).

Julian was before you.
He obeyed me like some monstrous Cleopatra
in miniature, as though I had the same
black hair and dark entrancing eyes.
I left Julian for you…
and you left me for Heidi,
all bouncy, blonde and debonair.

It didn't stop us from our onward journey,
swinging each other round
and around and around in gay array.

Only the playtime bell could end our adventure.
Once back in class we were forced to drink
bottled milk from white unbending straws.
It had an unusual bitter-sweet flavour,
... reminiscent... of the milk
that I still sometimes taste of yours.

Little Miss Bukowski Jr.

Jesus just like her father
seen in downtown New York City
reading at CBGB's
high on speed
in combination downers, poppers.

Falling over some loser
dishcloth mouth holding the drink
a two humped camel
pock mark smile
not so endearing on the iris.

Living somewhere at the bottom
not that you'd notice
fraying curtains, double locks
and 24 hour eviction clause.

Make sure it's quiet
when the men call round
historians, failed poets
swallow a line
then write it all down.

Could do with bathing more often
stinks of urine
you can't say it
she'll rattle snake slit
through the hole in your wallet
like the only one

even bet it's too late
for fingers tattoo'd brown.

Strange Fruit

He'd peer like Ivor Cutler over the counter
personal service for every customer

Yellow smile and matching nails
place each item in piles on the scales
with delicacy – cooking for two tomorrow?

Tomatoes, cauliflower, lemon for tahini,
okay half a cucumber one cut evenly.

A 999 wake up call
across the road their eyes stole
smoke wafting fresh out the jaffa king store

Watched him head on
steaming like an old gas stove
at the firemen
face and shop ashen
the sign above the door dirt brown.

Never to be swayed he opened at ten
instead of half eight that morning
couldn't miss the trade.

Oh Mr Jaffa King why your fruit so charred?

Message to a Friend

He knows
I am a troubled soul tonight.
My mind and body jangle,
in a constant state of flux,
unable to relax.

Friendship misunderstandings
left a sour taste
in my throat.
Disturbed and disconcerted,
ripped a dress apart,
torn and ruined.

Pat Metheny and Charlie Haden
in the background
do not
still anxiety.

The pretty throws
across the bed
are funeral flowers
of ruby red
from dark red blood
dripping from my legs.

Attempts to disembowel
this bitter ache
with an elegy.

Going to the Bottle Bank

Better move quick
off that best seat in the house
I'm going cheap see
there's plenty of me here
at two ninety nine
and thirty three per cent proof.

Forget the leccy, housework
that shave you were going to have
those January bills
and come and get
nine bottles of me
any less would be an insult.

Don't be slow now
I'm running out fast
you'll find me somewhere
way at the back
that Lara Croft shimmy
you've perfected for hours.

And take me there
to where I belong
burning the oesophagus
sloshing on the tongue.

She Limits Herself to Three Cigarettes

Can't sleep, popping powder for eternity
new year's resolution to quit
balanced on a dim lit concave refraction.

Doesn't help him kneading
urging symbiosis till he gives up
takes it personal and rolls like a boulder.

She goes to bed too soon, wakes too early
shouldn't sleep at all in the afternoon
stay up until the others are ready
her sleep patterns are simply odd, that's true
today he's doing good, getting plenty.

Head rock on the pillow
she sleeps straight through the eclipse of the sun
the brightest moon
the chemicals had a latent effect
saw it later on the news.

Downstairs they've vacuumed, done karaoke
sneezed several times, had a temperate argument
while she's that cushion on one corner of the mattress
with the hand crocheted cover on.

He wakes, a stolen moment
quickly she makes two coffees, spoons
brings them in but by then he's asleep again
back to her, a closed suitcase.

Calling Card

Sat in the rocking chair
reeling off religious poetry
ad-libbing over the top of the cds.

Melancholic Gerry setting my teeth on end
only came over to smoke all that weed
crumbling hydroponic single sensimilla bud
expecting silver service, serviettes
and a private chamber maid.

Strappelli can't you get rid?
have a word with one of your associates
carrying that plastic gun hold up in Woolworths
a rusty bread knife threatening
the home care woman and police.

You not in sat hours nun silent
juggling his shrinking balls in my palms.

Don't take this personally
it wasn't so directed
real sinners us two.

Hold the receiver up close friend
he'll return and next time
it could be you.

Generation X

For Al and Steve

He only want to be famous
don't be so hard on him
look at the track listings
in the small print
late night personal ad on tv.

He need his hot white daily intake
to guard off the shakes
keep his hand in rhythm and blues.
It's a jam nation
with mellow Leonard on the sausage roll
melancholic Gerry with a mouthful of blamange
stuffing it all in
and the leader of the African National Congress on lead.

Gerry said not to get so quimlistic
a fridge full of food out there in the kitchen
- Joy on tap to prepare it.
Leonard this year's sitting judge in parliament
signed the epigraph of hope and success
intent in this year's screenplay
wins at 8 to one and 3 to 2 on making tracks
on a cv of gambling aspirations.

Aims: nothing for the leccy bill
to bring joy, happiness
not even any lightbulbs in
to the world, a dress for the wife
toilet roll, trips to social services
fuck it, anything she wants
food parcels for the step kids
there's always something
don't be such a head fuck.

Said linguistically speaking
he's simply having an abreption
my only son thinks in mood vibes man
needs his red right hand, dreams and inebriation
first in line for the bullets
like John Lennon I'm the one

stuck in hill billy land
chinking paper cup promises
in a carrier bag screwed up
on the floor with all the other
bottles, cash and cigarette papers.

Notes

1   Fatalism
"because she was hoping for an early death" is a line from The Smiths song What She Said, on the Meat is Murder album, 1985.

2   Spaced, 1999
"First big weekend of the summer" is a phrase from the song of the same name by Arab Strap on the album The Week Never Starts Around Here, 1996.

3   Con Man
"bonsai aphrodite" is a phrase from the song Black Market Baby by Tom Waits on the album Mule Variations, 1999.

4   Lengths
"Big in Japan" is a phrase from the song of the same name by Tom Waits on the album Mule Variations, 1999.

5   Putting up the Relatives
Slapper Testing is a poem by Al.

6   Bastard Landlord.
consistuency: the vibe of a particular group of people.

7   Message to a Friend.
"Message to a friend" is the title of a track by Pat Metheny and Charlie Haden on the album Beyond the Missouri Sky, 1997.

8   Generation X.
The title is taken from the book of the same name by Douglas Coupland, 1991.

X facts: quimlistic = exaggeration
 abreption = nervous collapse (Steve & Al)

Don't Let Death Move In
Daithidh MacEochaidh

Contents

To ma Grandma, Mary Keogh, who can't read poetry
&
to Vicki McMaster who doesn't.

"We didn't have metaphors in our day. We didn't beat around the bush."

Trueman, F. Radio, see *Private Eye No. 905*

"If you don't fight death it will just move in."

Bukowski, C. *War All the Time – Poems 1981 –1984*
Santa Barbara, Black Sparrow Press

Norman Tebbit's Cycle

I didn't drink as a rule in *The Queens*,
the beer was crap and the pub dog
smelt of Horlicks, bad thing that, for a pub.

A man came in known to me
only very slightly, gave me a plastic-bag
primed with a Raleigh's bicycle pump.

He'd just tried to hold up the Post Office
on Newland Ave with it. It woh hot
and the police were heading him off at the pass.

When they nailed him
his defence was that it could not have been him,
for he had been down the *St John's*
trying to score some dope.

This lie didn't save him.
It been well known that Ethel
had barred him years ago
for exposing his tattoo of Winston Churchill.

He got three years,
did eighteen months,
met the ald charv' in *The Old White Hart*
wanting his now-tepid pump back.
I wasn't there, guv'ner,
I was down the *St Johns*
down on ma luck
trying to score some hope.

Oxford Street

Masel' and Mick Baines
were doing our best to by-pass
Oxford Street, trying to find this
Sam Smith's pub we'd stumbled over
the last time we were in London,
when Baines sank his cig-stained fingers
into us, fingers of smeared ochre
and burnt flesh, fingers any Egyptian
mummy wouldn't have been seen dead
wearing, them fingers delving in ma shoulder:
"Eh up, Prudames! Oliver Prudames!"

There larger than coincidence
was a lad well detested at school
for sniffing your underpants
during games; there we'd be
layking rugby while warm and dry
inside, Prudames with the permanently
bad cough and letter from his mother
would be at wrapping our duds around
his nostrils, inhaling for dear life,
nay wonder the fucker had a permanently
bad cold, snifferlus, we called it.

And there he was, in a nice suit
walking down Oxford Street as if
he owned it, walking on by, slight
sniff, condescending and insincere,
as he made it into the distance
without turning back, as we
called that whore's melt all the
bad words we knew and even a few
we didn't ken as Mick Baines

gave him the finger, a big, grimey
finger, almost gangrenous in colour,
abiotic as a fossilised turd: -
shit, I never got over that finger
and we never found our pub
and Prudames the Sniffer
looked to be doing well…
but that finger, man,
was another story entirely.

Well Tempered Claret in ABC Minor

Woke up this morning all covered in blood
like a fugue in a carpet searching for a blues song.
I felt tight and right and aching to do wrong
saving all my yesterday for far too long.

And there's so many ways you can get the Blues
is what Buddy Guy said this gig I heard
on my bootleg life – so many counterfeit fears,
eating up and burning up all down the years.

Yet it still felt strange to wake with such pain,
feeling the blood kick out through my veins,
and if I could I would and surely should
do all this and more yet again,

spraining both sides of my brain,
ordering, sorting, filing each crashing chord,
submerging tonics, working out sudden Dorics
of harmonics and to hell with the words.

It never added up,
this minor mode work-shop
pumping arterial forfeit,
a blind fugato in a carpet.

Mary Keogh has Burnt her Corsets

I don't know why but ma grandmother
hates the queen's mother with real vim
and vigour: this is not a poem,
but it meks mi laugh

Transmigration of a Potato

Prata, a tatie, seeded itsel'
by the tumbled walls,
small and coarse in ma hands,
rough with grit and toughened skin
protecting white heart of bland starch,
bitten raw, sharp as the salt of memory:

Port, Donegal, a village left to the waves,
three generations failed and left to wander,
(Britain, States, Canada)
far from the gull-sung blister of rocks.

Later, chewing on cooked potato,
having ma fill of famine stories
and the hatred of the English,
my hunger returned, sank into a frozen bite of memory,
grubby as the black earth caked in the nails of ma fingers
and not for shifting.

Focal Eile

to J – I'm reet sorry

I loved a girl for her neologism:
      gatheration,
though we did not meet
      that often.

Al Jolson's Blues

This whisper blew around the auditorium
accompanied by the usual exhortations
to shush and hush and don't you know Big Al is on?
I did and didn't care. The whisper was
that a doctor was needed.

I'm no doctor but I knew what was wrong.
Big Al was up front pleasing the white folks,
blacked up to the eyeballs and beyond,
calling for Mammy and a lynching.

I found him in his dressing room,
top billing no more, his blackness
fading as if they'd beaten the blackness
out of him – he was dying, going fast.

I pulled up a chair, removed the trumpet,
a mute stuck in its throat. His eyes gleamed a little
upon seeing the brass, but his trumpet was tinker-scrap.
I asked how it was, though I knew.

He was sorry, sorry so bad,
but he wasn't apologising, just explaining,
so I'd know that he'd never meant to end his life
auditioning for no Disney Cartoon caricature.

I nodded, stroked his hand, biting my lip.
He whispered, spittle and blood coming
to his busted mouth, *Those white
motherfuckers weren't worth blacking up for.*

Damn right. He was right as ever. I stroked his hand.
I cradled his big beautiful head I held it tight, tried not to see
tears falling. *See it was the only way, only way*
back then... He tried to speak, but a gobbit of blood filled his mouth.

From the auditorium came a wave of laughter.
Big Al had his banjo out now, cooning up,
sweating like a slave making his boot-polish run.
Inside the room I held his head so he couldn't listen no more.

He heard. He heard it all. Everything they said,
specially young left critics with all the answers
and no forgiveness and he didn't need no forgiveness,
not from nobody. He told me again that his mouth had gone.

I ran my fingers through the thinning mat of his hair.
They was snow in his hair. There was ash burnt into the black.
I ripped open my shirt. Held him to my breast and bid him feed.
He tried. Nothing but skin and bone, his lips had gone.

From the auditorium came raucous cheers, mad handclaps,
never ending shouts of encores – Big Al was giving it all
he never had, just stole. Inside the room he was dead.
I closed his eyes, but they wouldn't buckle down.

I was shewn out then. I'd done enough harm,
me and all my kith and kin. I walked away.
His friends, relatives, knelt down and prayed.
Inside Al's Coon Show was still playing strong –

Nigel

It wasn't his fault that he faked his headache, his orgasms, his membership of the Monday Club, then finally his death in tragic circumstances a tad outside Ashton-Under-Lyme. The insurance company paid up in full ten weeks after the funeral. The cheque bounced. What it is to give a man a bad name.

A Kind of Wedding

Idling ma time at *Lidle's*
waiting for Vicki to find a pound
for the trolley, and pulling
the underpants from the crack
of ma arse, when arrives
in the car-park the wedding
party, and eeeh, the bride looked
lovely, new dress and a tab
in her gob, and a husband
still sober, don't know what
they were doing there,
but there was this deal
on Heinz baked beans
and other bargains galore:
p'raps best start on't reet foot,
live cheap and save for' future.
Vicki pulled away with her trolley,
her pound, leaving me limping on
behind, eyeing the beans,
other bargains,
and open to offers.

Lecture Notes

Joshing apart there's this professor
      preaching his sermon in all seriousness
and there's mi-self following every move.
      This may look innocuous enough,
but looks ain't everything and I'm in Bremen
      to hear him go over one more time
all that stale ground, all that instability
      of the signifier, thinking that he
was making it up as he went along
      though I've heard it all afore,
and the end looms up all smiles and
      handclaps when I shouts, *Kundsheit*!
Some wag in the front row exclaims,
      ah Plat Duutch!
But I was wrong.

On that tour I followed that man everywhere:
      Hamberg, Hamlyn, Hangover, Hungry,
all the Haiches which is unusual as I tend to drop mine.
But in every lecture meine Professeur was on form
and I would shout, *Cutscheiss, Kunstshet* or some such slogan,
      but it made no difference.

I was wrong and my resolve was weakening,
      though the Euro looked dodgy,
I was in Beerlin, and I was a doughnut, and I had
      to have words at the end, just after muttering, *K-und-schite*,
he sought refuge in *Aldi*, but it was nay use:
      I told him what I really thought.
I was wrong, but I had had my say
      and in fairness he let me steal the show
in Glasagow: he sat still and bit the pill
      as I recited word-perfect-ly or some other

software package his lecture.
      At the end, everyone clapped and meine
Professeur congratulated me on my erudite
      delivery. I was wrong.

I walked away, but here's the thing that counts,
      outside there was this posse
of women, all with placards, all with
      my names spelt right;
all these angry women protesting against
      the language used –
At last, this was it, this was significant: now we were talking.

Pseud. Suede Shoelaces

It was the existentialists' millennium ball. God was playing dead again, true to type. But most people were too pissed to remember the rules. In the end, the butler did it with Mrs Scarlet in the broom cupboard with a candlestick. No one was that bothered. Not even Mr Scarlet who shot himself. God yawned.

The Great Chatsby

Ma mara swore blind that he had an option
on the greatest chat-up line in the 'bizzness'
and that, for a limited period only, I could
have a piece of the action — for a price.

Ma mara, being a master of cliché-ese
was almost always plausible, but I
wanted him to lay his cards on the table,
to lay it on the line one more time.

I followed ma mara for three nights solid
as he hit on the honeys with this line: -
he'd say, 'Hey, babe, don't I know you
from somewhere?' A lass would say, 'Nooooo!'
He'd say, 'I'm not talking about now,
I'm talking about the future.'
He got two black eyes, bust lips
and a nose spread generously about his face:
it was some punch-line.

I did not buy in while the price was right
on his once in a lifetime option chat-up line.

That's it, except to say I saw ma mara
moving in on some lass who did not
look to be in 'bizzness', corporate securities,
futures markets, or high risk venture capital,
but just leaned against the bar minding
her own drink. He said, 'Yo, babe, don't I know
you from somewhere?' She said,
'Chuffing heck, not you again!'

The Good Sex Guide to Adult Toilet Training
Parts 1 and 2

So Maria moved in,
I was nay too sure 'bout this at the time,
and by the way, don't be fooled
by the name, she not Spanish
or Latin or even Catholic,
she from the land of choirs, saunas
and more lakes than you could dishonestly
shake a stick at, and I was nay too sure,
but we bin ganning steady fe six years
come the anniversary of her last divorce.

She move in and after 3 days and 3
nights she telling me that we got a problem,
we had something that needing talking about –
right! And she takes me to the bathroom,
could have bin worse, her X she took to the
cleaners – I still see that man on a Satdee
selling *The Big Issue*. So we in the clodgy,
wi' the seat position up, top and seat thing
pointing to heaven.

She said, Man, this in't gud enuff this day
and age – seat goes down, Man! You sexist
Bastard! I'm a bit non-plussed about all
this, but I check with mi friends who just
happen to be girls about what's going down
and they on her side to a man. Anyroad,
I'm a bit pished abart all this happening
in the throne room, saying, look this is all
pot luck: I go it's up, you go it's down, equality –
and when I take a crap you getting an extra down –
you gaining on this woman!

Tee-pee-cal, Man, she sorta sneers; Man defines
the concepts – equality?! You think phallocentricity
is all your dick! Look, Busta,
it is me or the John! she saying and meaning it.

So I takes one look at the clodgy and one look
at the pout on Maria and I know it's no contest,
perhaps she having a point after all, perhaps
I am sexist, built that way.

So okay the next day, me gets these six
inch nails and super-glue for the loo
and I baton down the hatches. So

one morning she catches me using her
herbal toothpaste and it's curtains. She moving out
and the next thing me hears she moving in
with this drunk x-docker who beats up on her
and has Venetian Blinds.
As for me and John? We're solid.
We're still steady. Maybe
this is for life.

Made for Walking

All last Sunday, he trained his pedigree retriever to tie his shoelaces. The dog became confused when it came to the flip-flop, the Wellington boot and the humble slipper. After ganning on strike, Rover, got parity. He still ties shoes. And the owner is learning how to bury a bone. The wife walked away, barefoot.

Dice Work If...

I guess I'm no longer playing *Ludo* by post with
the *Broadmoor* inmate; the Prison governor, no less
sent me the news with an official stamp on it, offering
me an ageing neurotic instead and his condolences, saying that
yon man had hung hissen. I'm green, allus green, to change the
subject, my Orange Brother-in-law maintains that it's the
Fenian coming out in me, but bugga that for a game of soldiers – as
the mighty poet Mike Harding said at this gig that time me working
down in the smoke, seeking a neet of Northern comfort, anyroad
that's not the issue here, and by the way, yon man woh allus red
and not for any carnal or carnage archetypal reasons, just 'cos it
woh his mam's, Queenie's, favourite colour. *The Red and the Green*:
sounds nigh on gud enuff for a book cover, and I guess this postal
playing of *Ludo* was quite novel: one move a day, though sometimes
a move wud gan astray in't post and Christmas wud be a reet bugga,
yon man lost three moves, 3 strikes, in a row and neva really recovered.
But can't mek sense of his quitting, specially this game; all his
counters were lined up already, all he needing woh one man back
in the block, this blank cell waiting on a lucky three to win.
I still had one man half-ways round an' another stuck
in the holding pen, hoping on a super 6 to set him free.
Guess, I'll neva ken his jacking in and summart else an' all,
I'll miss that owd fecker, maugre crimes and sins,
the things he did. All day, me carrying this grief around till
I get out the board, set the pieces, throw the die, shek
that missing six, then a four, then play for yon man who sheks
a five, a bust the way we layke, then I shek
a two…Suddenly, there's this choice, move mi back
marker or wi' mi front man nobble the red;
I can send that red token all the way back –
a choice, a chance, to catch up, but…
can you punish a dead man?

I sit, wireless on, something rather refined on 3 from York's
Early Music Festival, do I get the man? do I play the gentle-
man? or shit on the bastard and play the game? Brumel's
Magnicat Secundi Toni, torn in twain, playing for and against
this dead man, get to wondering, is this the moment when
madness firsts sets in? Pick up counter. Mek a move.
The die is cast — *alea jacta est* —
just too late, allus too late.

Tensed

Somewhere, a horse leads a man to water. It tasted like lead, sat rather heavily on the horse's stomach. The beast had the sense to walk away, somewhere, leaving the man thirst-quenched though lost. When they found his horse, somewhere, they sold it for scrap. The widow was grateful for the money. The man drank.

Sir Oswald Mosely's Seat of Government

At Sotherbys on Saturday despite being the Sabbath
Sir Oswald Mosely's underpants were ganning under the gavel.
They had aroused a lot of interest in and from certain quarters:
communists/Tories, liberals/labour and dangerous White Supremacists
from the Southern Estates of the East End – after all these pants
had been around a bit, liberal jocks that had gone to bed with anyone,
clapped themselves to more than one vacant seat, a legend in their own
bedtime be damn.

They were held up and not for ridicule as the auctioneer opened the bidding
with a big one, then beefing up the price by informing the public on the
whys and wherefores of Mosely's y-fronts, though tastefully refraining
from mentioning how they had dropped a bollock climbing
into the bunker with Hitler; this long afore the art of spin-doctoring
could put a patch, stick on a sound-bite, on such tissues
of photo-opportunism at a de-briefing session.

The bidding was steady. The auctioneer threw in the towel
just to boost the juice on the sale, going through the motions
of going once, twice, going like a train, when he banged his gavel
down and the pants spanked into action wrapping themselves
around the gavel, the stick hitting the upper seam,
can't keep a good man down it seems:
the bidding got out of hand, all the president's men were in town –
pants were destined stateside till the Prime minister rose from his coffers
coughed up the readies for Mosely's shreddies, a bargain buy after all
the shenanigans of the Displeasure Dome.

I didn't stick around for the job-lot on Prescott's surgical truss,
the Lady's not for turning g-string or even Paddy Pants-down's
game contribution, as the cries from the fitting room proved too
distracting, the PM having a bad pubic hair-day, no doubt,
as the turncoat cabinet queued along behind, eager as rats
leaving a sinking shit, though they barred Mo Mowlem

for having ministerial ability and a sense of humour…
As I say, I left. The spin-doctors were back in as the judge
banged his gavel down three Christ-denying times:
history – pants
politics – pants
poetry – the biggest pants of all,
as they brought in Yeats' fabled duds,
cut sleek as a Free-State Blue-shirt
with a thinly disguised reversible Butcher's Apron sewn in on the inside –
it was a national treasure, but which nation, no one knew…bargain!

26/09/00

Woke up this morning
pulled back ma bedroom curtains
found a dead pigeon on ma kitchen roof -
don't sound like a Blues Song,
but I still feel bad about it – oh yeah!

After Hours

For the ladz at the Parsonage

My mate's dad
used to come home
after the pubs shut
and argue in the kitchen
with nobody.

I did one better in a Jazz club
in Amsterdam, arguing all night
with nobody
as they still brought me drinks,
and nobody cared.

Holland is very liberal like that.

Angry Dolphins

She told me
she was into Wicca.
I told her
I fancied female Vicars.

She said she worshipped the moon above,
frenzied foreplay and free love.
I said I weren't going to pay for it anyway.
She said, Fuck off, mate, it ain't your lucky day.

We picked organic magic mushrooms together
in *Playaway* Day-Glo dungarees and inclement weather.
It just wasn't that hip jumping ship mid-bad trip,
to find she'd dumped my Tom Waits CDs in next door's skip.

I saw her again in Glastonbury
driving this brightly painted under 3-tonne lorry.
I'd hitched in with hikers and bikers
and under-aged bare-knuckle fighters.

She had two kids, two dogs,
and made a living selling hand-knit gollywogs.
She said she missed me like gallstones,
a burst appendix and bagpipe overtones.

I just couldn't be sorry
when she left in her lorry,
knowing that hate was thicker
than Wicca or a cross-dressing Sunday school vicar.

Food for Thought

I was scratching at the scars of ma full frontal lobotomy, nails packed with clotted thoughts and the remains of memory when ma head fell off just as the bus came with room for one on top. Odd, not having the right change or, even, a head to call ma own; bite ma nails, pensively.

Crack-Out

When the crack cocaine hits his brain
he feels no pain, content to sit out
the dark, listening to her crying,
finding little lips in her tears
contoured to her cheek unable
to mouth the name of any exit out.

When the crack cocaine hits his brain
he lip-reads numb from the skull down,
fumbling the room's Braille for something
signifying an opening, an ending, a way out –
the writing on the wall perhaps
or the graffiti of tears checking out.

Clean-Hands Chucky Armani

For Dan the Man MacCauley

He came from Monaghan,
I don't know if that's an issue
or not, or even relevant,
but he would stand at the bar
drinking or ordering a pint,
willie out and the piss flying.

He could talk politics this man,
the names of the ancient heroes
of Erin's green isle, he could wile
away afternoons at the bookies
without a care in the world,
but he couldn't keep his flies up,
in the pub, buying the round,
great gouts of Fenian piss
dissing the place, and
he never washed his hands
in public.

The 518 to Newcastle

for Kamau Brathwaite

Brathwaite, man, I ken
you don't see the ruling classes
at the bus stop, but I wouldn't want
to see 'em, bags in ma hand hoping
for a seat this time, let the sods walk:
the minister for transport walking
barefoot in the sun.

I don't want to see the cabinet
the next time I'm fighting to get
to the bar down at ma local boozer,
when I need that drink, the sup
of the friendly stuff, to put the big
fat painted smile on the battered
clown's arse of face ma life wearing.

I don't want to see the minister
of health as I'm helping ma marra
Baines find a decent vein left
for a spike of heroin. I don't want
that ras lecturing, hectoring
getting in the way,
as this could be the charva's last
fix and he could die happy.

I don't want to see the minister
of justice as I'm left humping
ma right hand 'cos the woman
that loves me, can't bear me
touch her after all them rapes
she took when but a girl-child,
fucked and nothing but a pickney,
that minister for justice,
that scunt don't show his face
near that girl's pain.

It's ma stop,
the bus running late
and I don't want to see
no ruling class here,
I don't want them bunch,
of cunts in ma life,
I want 'em dead, Kamau,
        me want 'em dead.

Lark. Curlew.

Ah thowt nowt te hear
the curlew screm
as ah stalked the moor
of mi mind,
whilst abuv, in yon slip of heaven,
skylark woh yam'ring
song, brittle and shrill -
a vain piping,
an' on fynding its scrip o' nest
o' wan grass and breast-feather med,
ah replaced each egg wi' cald stoan
as mishappen as mi ain thrawn mood,
each egg still warm te't tuch
'eld the pip o' unformed eye,
brimming fresh seeght an' morn's new song,
but what woh that te mi as ah stalked
empty moor of mi mind
hearing yon curlew scream.

Bets are in

I never made it to the Galway Races.
I made it to the pub, watched 'oss
after 'oss just pacing round,
on an old black and white portable,
only two or three trying each race.
My turn at the bar.
I didn't hurry.
The barmen placed the bets
by phone and Tom Cullan
won a ton and said he'd stand
a double round.
It was my turn at the bar.
I didn't hurry.
I drank a Guinness and a double
Powers on your man Tom Cullan.
Sometimes I'm a cunt like that,
and those 'osses just coasting round,
I wonder what they're drinking?

Facing up the Years

For you see, he would see the child,
a dab of spit, tired hanky, moving circles
buffing up his boots, clear reflection,
that bairn's face, eyes shut.

It got so bad one time he felt like giving it
all up, retire to the country, some country,
out there amongst dark smudge of pines,
child's face in his medal, Patriots' Day.

Some whiles, late at night maybe, sipping foreign whiskey,
he'd kill it with his cronies, mother, even you too,
lie about it all, figuring some other's way,
this child he saved and flipping the other side of his face.

He never dreamt but could see tugging, pulling
sitting upon his knee that child, broken leg swinging,
talking him back from all he had, all he did,
not having the time to listen, so looking back, looking ahead.

None of it was any good, couldn't matter, putting his face on bank notes
when they said at last he'd died. Statues in marble, statues
of granite and the grey, grey concrete when times were hard.
Taking, trapping, deep stone down, some child's face, eyes shut.

Advice

"I'm really tired of coming to readings,
hearing nothing but bad language,
plain prose disguised as poetry, full of
aberrant sexual practices and drug-abuse;
tired and sick of it all," said ma critic.
I told 'im, "Stop at home then, lad,
get your head down for an early night."
He walked away, unenlightened.
He did not buy a copy of ma book.

Well Told Lies

Everything that I say here
or there
or perhaps just
anywhere

is lies, but more than lies
this is bullshit
and no holds barred.

But I warned her,
of that I insist
is true as I sidled up to the bar
and put in my order for a beer
or two, she asked me what I
do and I told her straight
that I specialised in lies
her mouth dropped and she raised
her eyes, said that she could believe
that, but in truth wanted some kind
of proof, anyone can tell a pork pie now

so she believed my bullshit
and there was nothing left to do
but to try to come clean, lay it
on the line: "I'm a psycho-head-case
scrounging on the bru, I shouldn't drink
but do and wile away the hours
at home improving seven different strains
of mould with which to take over the world –
I'm winning too, kitchen and bathroom
are already through."

She laughed got in the beers,
said she liked wee witty men, cos they
try so much harder. I said, "If I see any,
I'll let them know."
It was then that she asked me really

what I do. Biting my lip, stemming
tears I told right from the start,
getting kicked out by Maria, finding my
only son out fishing along the river
with my wife's latest lover, living
in a flee-pit, trying to gain some kind
of hold on what was left of my assets, the yacht,
apartment in the Maghreb and that Swiss
bank account no one was supposed to know
about.

I broke off, said it was my shout.
Got in the beers as she dried her
tears, took her home to meet the mould.

Now we sit, hand in headlock, in
unholy wedlock, not knowing
the difference between the prosaic
and the Prozac, or swilling down
large doses of Haloperidol
with cheap, Bulgarian Vino,
every day me waking with
some new tale, some new lie, to light up
our lives, my girl, my sweet woman,
she on more medication than would
kill a raging bull and I tell you,
tell you all, allyou,
that this,
this bullshit
is
for real
for life
for ever.
I tell you this from the heart,
ask yourselves
would I lie to you?

Porgy Lost Buckra

to the memory of Michael Smith who danced to his own drum, only

Buckra searched the markets for a new minstrel. He wanted to hear those old songs again performed to a cakewalk, shake and shuffle, clink-clink of ankle bracelets, spread as thick as good quality jam. Today's minstrels just couldn't cut the make-up, refusing to sing and dance, despite offers of equity cards, ludicrous publication details and copious mentioning on Wireless 4 to 3 – it was a right bloody performance. Buckra despaired till late one sable-black, bible-black night, he caught a bit of that darkness all to himself, rubbed it in skin-deep and seeing nothing in the mirror he capered and danced to an invisible audience of 'other' Buckra, polished for the part, mere background artists merging into the night. Buckra don't need no Porgy – Buckra is his own master now.

Blas

Crazy Durcan would visit his father's cows
with a small three-legged stool to milk his cock,
never minding the flies or shit or various Biblical
injunctions against that sort of thing entirely and not
to be eating prawns too, mind, if you're going
that way on, and he never did fuck a pig,
interestingly, so the Old Catholic
Guilt must have been good for something,
though he would never cry when his beloved
cows went for slaughter, 'Bring the next fecker!'
he'd roar, his milking stool tucked into his oxter.

Going to Meet the Man

Ah went te see 'im,
not that it woh advised,
but ah med that journey -
te see the man;
this man wi' dribbled smiles
fe no one particular,
amazed that strangers wud cum
ev'ry day te spoon-feed 'im,
mashed up this and that
or clean 'im up,
wash his genitalia.

From his winda seat
ova looking ' grounds
he cun't guess that
he living naw in-a 'ospital.

Strangers cumming ev'ry day
checking his pulse, sometimes
piping in his bladder - strange sensation.
These people, these strange blank faces,
wud pull a blanket ova him when
it grew cowd, reet cald - just
dead-bone coald inside.

They advised mi not te go,
not te mek that journey after all
this time and all that had gone on;
all that unalterable past atween us.
Ah ganned, took one deek
at t'auld man an' kent full well
that all t' questions I had weren't
werth spit, not naw.

So ah held his hand
fe a wee while,
drank the pish-warm tae
till it woh time te walk away.

All there is, is teXtosterone

They got 'em by the short and curlies, all signifiers that wouldn't toe the party line, beyond semantics, beyond semiotics, beyond the obsolete 11+ even. They gave 'em no either/or or neither/nor or a golden handshake for all that hard graft they had put in. They just robbed 'em blind of their chance-found ikonic status.

Blood till Thursday

Ma Uncle Tom had never seen so much blood,
not even after losing two rifles in Korea,
as when his uncle and father
slaughtered a deer up in Launton Woods
and carving it up in the back kitchen;
a strike was on, nay one working;
this is nay poem about hard times back then,
but this now after John Slater's rabbit
squats at ma feet, small knife in ma hands,
small pool of blood in the backyard,
hoping that the wee coney will last
till Thursday's dole cheque gamely
flops onto ma doormat as all the deer
in Thrunton Woods breathe a sigh
of poor relief as Peter Rabbit
tubthumps on a toadstool that
it's high time Mr MacGregor
culled the poor, as Bambi
re-loads a chance-found rifle:
praise Pan and pass the ammunition.

...the Biscuit

I bought this "No Frills
Jamaican Ginger Cake"
and they weren't lying.
I bought it to cheer masel' up
and it didn't; it really woh
the real McCoy "No Frills".
There was a Catholic Priest
I knew whose greatest thrill
was hearing Sean O' Se sing
Do Bhi Bhean Uasal/Carrick Fergus
in both English and Irish –
it was that sort of parish.
I could believe ma next door
neighbour when she said
that her greatest thrill
after her husband leaving her
was the buying of a fourteen
inch double intruder.
I could believe ma mate's greatest thrill,
a born again political animal,
was the seeing, late at night, of
the non-election of Miguel Portillo.
I can believe ma dog's greatest
thrill is worrying our postman
as he pushes through the circulars,
letters and bills. I just don't ken
what is ma biggest thrill,
but I just know it ain't
this f-ing Jamaican Ginger Cake.

Losing It

for P.T. McT. yu knaaw that death's not sudding wurth it

Everyone said that Steve had lost it.
They were wrong. Steve hadn't
lost it the way Dee lost it that time,
taking him away, taking the knife off him
and him thinking that every Jinnah was out
to rape him and some hard-nuts down
Tang Hall way had a contract out to take him out.
No way Steve was in any shape like that, but...
but I kent the lad had it bad.

His mother bad me go over to try and talk
it through, all of it. Didn't think I stood
a chance, it couldn't be done, wouldn't
help a damn, but...
but I went; least I could do.

So, I get to find Steve in the bath, but
not the way your thinking, probably.
There's this scolding hot bath, full of suds,
bath-oil, baby bath and *Persil Xtra* something or
other that's kind to your clothes and does nay
hurt the environment too. Steve was bathing,
doing his washing and for a while there
even cleaning his teeth with this pale-blue flannel.

For a while there we didn't say an awful lot,
nothing that meant anything to him or me,
just some phatic phrase hoping to get the
talk flowing. And then, then, Steve asked me
if I thought that he was mad. No way, Jose,
I said, putting on this mad Mexican bollocks of an accent,
as I assured him that I too had dhobied ma washing
in the tub when I had no machine of ma own or money

for the launderette or one of my pairs of odd socks
woh smelling bad – Steve had laughed at that,
things couldn't be so bad.

He cried a little then, then
asked mi a favour, asking me
to soap and scrub his back.
I got the soap, lathered up,
found the brush and scrubbed
as he told me about it, about that
wife of his, this man she working
with at work who incidentally is
getting on just fine with Steve's kids;
last time he seeing Susan and Joe
they not wanting to know their father
from shit – just the way it goes, bro,
he saying, trying to say, crying.

Scrub the back, he wanting me to
scrub his back one more time, but
the soap gone, just mush and dissolve,
something suddenly stinging the eyes –
know too, back there in that bathroom,
I, me, I, woh losing it too.

Don't Look at me with those Words

to the memory of Ian Dury, a beautiful spastic full of wit
& don't give a fuck, who took no shit

It was Spaka Day in town
and there was little point
getting prosaic about it –
that's what they called it,
the local, the local, fuckwits;
every Wednesday, they'd bring in
the crips, the spaks and spazzaz,
the drivelling loons and twitching nuts:
it passed the time.

Locals got used to it,
appreciated the custom,
the patronage, it was
good to see 'em
struggling to get off
the mini-bus;
every shop some warm
welcome and how're doing.
All the locals looked,
looked forward to seeing
spades they called a spades,
and they never had a dig
or made a nudge
or a wink-wink:
they saw what they saw
they wouldn't look
away, politely
and they said
what they said
and thought nay worse of it.

And their audience?
The folk that came
week after week
to gawp at shop-keeps,
tradesmen/women,
bar-keeps and café
owners, these people,
they too liked the look
of Bedlam, looking
ahead to the ungainly,
unfolding of the week.

Meister Eckhardt's Epistemological XTC

You put tabs on mysticism
sell them on street corners or a certain pub's clodgy,
but allus somewhere under t' counter:
strawberries but never raspberries,
snort that 'oss not te Banbury Cross
and allus double flush te get the most
from your spike. Start in
on those colours, prescribe solutions
te that auld formulation of distinctions
atween primary and secondary qualities,
except there's no quality control
with this shit though it's said that at
gigs in Amsterdam there's chemists
on call to unravel and inform on
the formula, though that's maybe cheating
unlocking the mysteries that could put
you in a fix, so act dumb instead,
take plenty of H_2-Ho!-Ho!-Ho! and
have a machismo laugh about
all this, stick spurs in Oss and
ride that night-mare te Banbury Cross,
when you get there enter despair,
fumbling fe words, concepts, bricks and bones
of words, consonants and vowels, phonemes,
p-possibly some gently plosive, but you gotta
say something, sometime:
O Wort, du Wort,
das mir fehlt!'"
It's all words, slung together, propping up
a sentence signifying nothing, the texture of
text, distinctly lacking, never mind the actualities of
ontological textuality, printed word paper thin. But
Meister Eckhardt is getting there, he's a whiz,
a couple of grams of the Tetragrammation in

solution is no problem.
He knows now, he really kens:
it's like he's gone to bed
wi' the Godhead –
Vereinigt mit Gott.
He knows:
gnosis
g-no
k-now
know
just say,
"No".

House of Words

for Mat

Ps invited me over to stay for a few days,
which sounded brave but wasn't as
when I went round he was not only not
in, but had moved last week. Still,
the man of the house bid me stay a while
if I had nothing else on like, which I hadn't,
so all's well that started swell, said the
prostitute to the sailor or some other idiom
aspiring to cliché status – you know how it is.

On the second day of my stay, yon man
apologising for sleep-walking. None of mine
business, yon man, feel free to walk the Pennine
Way whatever time of the day you like, but I do
object to you wearing my Marx and Frank Spencer's
boxer shorts – clean on mind, from last Tuesday;
present from mi Grandma last Christmas – I said,
but I didn't like to nag.

On the third day he pulled on mi coat
about something or other, which was a tad
uncanny as it was hung over the banister
at the time, just minding its own business:
stocks and shares and negative equity
in the North of England again – that sort
of thing. Anyway, he said that he wanted
it known that he objected and had always
objected and left it at that, which didn't
leave me much room to make conversation,
especially as I was in the small downstair's
clodgy at the time applying my pile ointment.

Fourth day came along, smuggled atween
the third and fifth and starting mild enough,
though there's a promise of ground-frost for
the weekend, just so you know, when yon man
starts blubbing all by himself. He looked so lonely,
so I goes over and gives him a hand: just two quick
sniffles and a wipe of the eye or two, including
glass one, which was a good job as it was looking
dusty, and they don't come cheap these days.

Fifth day saw yon man no better, but then again
no worse as far as anything goes, which it
didn't as there was a corporation bus strike on
and not a wind to stir the washing, though still
no sign of the frost, thanks be to God. Anyway,
I thought he'd kicked the bucket, but he was
only shewing me it, said it was all she gave him
afterwards like to have, to hold to stick
in the rubbish bin. It wasn't his decision, he decided
after, but thought it a good idea to support her
none the less, but more none than less, and a
nod's as good as a wink to a guide dog, be God.

On the sixth day, he took the bucket for a walk
by the woods despite the ground frost, and I tagged
along too, still trying to get my boxer's back, not
that I'm right bothered, but a principal is not a
principle as my old Headmistress used to stress,
and she knew all the Latin words for the points
of the compass and had a nervous breakdown
whilst not been a member of the AA, though
she supped a fair bit in her spare time. Anyroad,
he saw some kids layking by ' park, stuck out his
thumb and said, see what I mean? I didn't
and anyway, what was the point of sticking out
your thumb with a bus strike on.

On the last day, we just mulled about all day,
doing damn all and arguing about slang in scrabble,
burning the Yorkshires, taking it easy, playing God,
with cheap Spanish wine and thin-sliced white bread.
But yon man got bored and buggered off to bed. I let
myself out and the cat in, promised to do it all again
sometime, wandering home watching the frost fall.

God's First Throw of the Dice for Albert Einstein

And today at the fall of evening
you invest the night, the uncentred earth
in constant uncertainties, past the days
unsure in their first tryst and turnings.

Nevertheless, you come awake with that one thought
that still unrests you, urgent, charming,
a forsaken token of domestic mourning,
looming out of the fog, forever.

In the tail of a comet
in all that burning spiral
of disintegrating iced light, you travel
back to a point, distant haphazard, moment.

Yet, memory, soberly masculine, robs the litter
of infinity, guilty as a vet's scalpel,
the street abortionist's dirty knitting needle,
and the steel syringe of convention.

You know there is someone still
looking for you, past all day and night.
You lie, but you still hold tiny, emptied shoes
impossibly small in your hands - they shake like dice.

You know there is someone, somewhere quietly rotting
in your pieces and part too of the one you left.
You see your quiet grief again in the forgotten corner
of that Swiss patent office, between the in-tray and the out.

You remember that woman's bravery, the thoughts
you once dared to share. And how she walked away,
made quiet all reproach, even later, even later,
after all that you did; all that did.

This is the real story...perhaps
You will die and everyone will say what/who you were.
They shall take your work and not understand it, pervert
it, turn it into their own re-writes. This is as it should be.
Others will try to tell the past as coherent, for a while

learning nothing,
never disputing the bias of perspective, the universal
constant, lightning, rain, the empty ether and the moving train.
They may demand in loud authorial voices, for your bones.
They may find you, finally. Lost

in some cold shouldered graveyard,
a time, an epoch's child, farmed out and orphaned.
They may demand your re-birth in history,
reassess whom they called, "a great man - genius."

You must have done something crazy to promise
such emotion back then. You are the new brute truth,
hungry as a torn throat. You marvel how your body
functions efficiently - but this can be despised too.

You find yourself in the fall of evening
a lost girl's hand tugging ancient frock-coat.
Cup your hands, shake, shake hands and wish,
then roll, scatter tiny shoes to gravity.

Your thoughts are united to its frame tonight.
You stoop, pick up the dice once more, wipe off dust,
cry a little perhaps: it is past, it is past.
You never got to ride a light-beam. Go on in, the night is cold.

Charlie Williams' Flat Cap

A boozer, under-age, some man
in a Rasta tam tekking the piss
out of Charlie Williams, calling
him an Uncle Tom or worse.
I've got an Uncle Tom –
nowt like the man.
Comedy was changing,
a laugh was something you
got intellectual about,
indignant about, but
nowt to laugh about.
Charlie had a smile that lit your heart,
his accent homely as ma gran's who
did laugh when Charlie
teld tales agin himsen,
or Yidz or thick Micks:
but Charlie didn't deserve
what that veggie, right-on
Rastaman woh giving him.
Prince Ras would have laughed,
that Semite, despot,
scion of Solomon, feeding
raw steak to his pet lion
would have laughed
at that black man,
laughed at our Charlie, if he could
have understood his proper Yorkshire,
but then agen that proud African King
never thought he woh black,
never thought he woh Jesus Christ either
or wore a tam or skanked
and spliffed. He was not that
sort of disposed dictator.
And I ain't having a pop

at the Rastaman, I'm
having a pop at him
having a pop, 'cos it
different now as then.
And when, all this pop
dies down and lies down flat,
Charlie lad, put on thy flat cap,
promenade proud as any African
autocrat along the strand at Scarborough,
and laugh, mate, laugh —

Connections

I once caught ma father
crying by the phone,
teld mi that mother
weren't coming back,
she'd left us
for a bandy-armed
cricketer,
there were real tears
in his eyes,
but ma sister and I
couldn't tell
if they were
of relief or sadness,
the phone was a real
piece of 70's merchandise,
all crappy purple plastic
and wrongly shaped
for chin and hand.
The 70s passed,
we got a new phone,
father left for London,
mother came back,
I moved in today
at ma new gaff,
it's pretty bari,
but for the 70s
phone left by the previous
owner, now resting in a home,
rang ma newly x-girlfriend
on it, just to say hello,
goodbye and to milk
a tear or two,
just to see
if I were still
connected.

A Taste of Mourning

I ate cold rice pudding that morning,
a spot of strawberry jam, burning off-centre
and the spoon from South Korea
tasting mellow metallic in my mouth.

My neighbour for these last three years
died in her sleep that night.
Her daughter called as usual at half
past eleven. You could hear her cry.

It was a small family funeral.
I could not find any worthwhile
words to say to her daughter or son.
I had bought flowers for the grave.

I have new neighbours now.
A young unmarried couple,
given to rows and much laughter
and who once invited me for dinner.

Over badly cooked vegetables,
stewed of taste, texture and flavour
I let slip the death of that old lady,
her daughter's cry seeping through walls.

On a fine day the man was hanging
out the linen-washing to dry on the wind,
so white in the spring sunshine, yet
a trace of spotted menstrual blood,
already marking out time.

The Put Down

"Don't give me that six counties shit!"
said ma mate Dai Bach to this well-
heeled lass from Surrey. Now Dai
had won the York Open Most Passionate
Welshman Contest three years running,
the only other contender that came near
was his brother, Tudor, beaten by a crisp.
But anyway, he'd meant the Home Counties,
not that the lass was bothered, thought
Hadrian had built Offa's Dyke and Dai Bach
was from the Czech Republic
studying town planning. She left him to it
and all, though she did agree that
there should be greater integration
in Europe, that the EC should be
expanded, as for the folk in the
Six Counties and Northern Ireland,
it was all Greek to them.

Chromatography

for David Morley

Uncle Tom's father came
from Barnsley to Scunthorpe
in a Vardo seeking work.
Following the road, working,
spreading the black stuff,
the degree that made ma
grandparents proud, lagging
lame at ma side like
some cast aside lurcher
too old to bring aught for the pot,
the tang of tarmac alive as a wasp
drone singing in my nose
as ma skin burns brown and tans,
feeling good and strong
and glad to be working,
and the Roma, the Rom Rayahs and Rawnees
travelling now, make it on the same
coach I travelled from Prague,
the sweet stink of Monika ground into ma skin,
that lally tchai's hair, burning ginger,
touch of red, against tight, black curly hair,
snug as a louse, travelling buckshee;
spreading the black stuff in the hot sun,
preparing an old road, puro drom,
knowing that it's time to nash
to kick ma crippled dog to work,
taking up the grudge fight
between impressionism and realism,
reff'ed by out-manoeuvred, out-moded modernism,
spit on the white popping blisters of my hand,
work ma tar brush into the fabric of the surface,
making a bari job of the road ahead.

Simon Sez

Simon sez, touch your toes
Simon sez, don't pick your nose
Simon sez, give good head
Simon sez, get into bed

Simon sez...

Simon din't say, cry
Simon don't have to say, why
Simon sez, keep it quiet
Simon sez, it's our secret

Simon sez...

Simon sez, he believes in the Holy Ghost
Simon sez, he believes in nothing but the truth
- the whole truth, nothing but, Simon sez
Simon sez, not guilty, not even close

Simon sez...

Simon sez, this is not a joke
Simon sez, purse your lips
Simon sez, have you done this before?
Simon sez, hands on hips

Simon sez...

Simon sez, not guilty
Simon sez, this is your God speaking
Simon sez, nothing but his truth
Simon sez, his prayers every night

Simon sez...

Simon's said enough

Some Strange Comfort

She looked like a library assistant
or possibly some minor civil servant
tucked away in an air-conditioned office –
I could have been correct, but wasn't.

We'd meet in the park,
throw crumbs to the sparrows
or those grey squirrels,
brave enough to creep close.

She did not meet my mother
of that I am sure.
It was not that sort of
relationship.

Most weekends we would have sex.
I never knew where she lived.
She would stop the night,
bringing only a toothbrush.

One day she was not there,
neither were most of my possessions:
my Jazz collection, computer and
the old black and white photograph
of my grandfather's village
in its cracked wooden frame.

I took clean socks and underwear
from a drawer, found a bag for a book
took also a toothbrush and locked up,
posting my keys through the door,
walking away at last, not looking back,
wishing this stranger some good luck.

Red Beautes

for Stephen Hopwood

She talked like she had someone else's plums
in her mouth, she lingered over her vowels
like a dirty old man I saw once in Marx's
fingering the lingerie like a connoisseur.
She said there was nay money for the reading
but would I settle for ma bus fair.
I would. I remembered a blues man,
doing a gig in London for a bottle of whisky
and a takeaway prostitute; Muddy Waters,
I told her about Muddy Waters and the gig,
and she said she'd try to get me a beer tab.
Big mistake, did the reading, got drunk,
fell in the gents and sprained an ankle,
took the last bus home, knowing it woh
really Howling Wolf that time in London,
and wished like hell that it had been
my plums that woman mouthing,
got off at ma stop, howled at the all-night milkman:
that's the Blues, that's the real Blues, Muddy —
cheap beer, nay woman
and a bad dose of fruit-envy.

What Harbour Shelters Peace?

They wouldn't bat an eyelid at Peter Grimes
in Amble, the friendliest of ports,
you can go slap-happy,
suffer accidental circumstances,
go gently mad, drinking the day
into the weeks and pick up
a bargain at the Sunday Market,
a big bag of kippers for a couple
of quid, if Britten had discovered
the North East, Peter Grimes
wouldn't've been guilty,
nay one would bother to fish
at these prices, and as for the
borough, they take all sorts here:
a stunted poet,
in his cups, liking his new digs,
the village, smuggling laudanum
into his midnight cocoa,
without a wife or bairn to be said to beat
and not making a song and dance about it
— land ahoy there, mates,
         land ahoy.

This poem has not been funded
by the Northumbrian Tourist Board.

Somekind

Back one time in The London
I was skanking to Reggae at a party,
when this Skin with beef and braces
asked me if I was some kind
of Nigger. "We all are; every
one of us made that walk out
of Africa at one time or another."
That was when he tried to bottle me.
I gave up dancing, discovered Radio 3,
and reading, and wearing John Craven's
cardigan. A different crowd altogether,
though Birtwhistle can get a bit rowdy.
I gave up dancing, pub-philosophy
and a hands on approach to politics
but not on being some kind of Nigger.

Grudge Match

The Jehovah Witness and the smartly dressed
American Mormon, brown suit and slicked back hair,
were fighting it out for ma doorbell
and din't I think masel' cute stuff
to be getting such attention, even when it turned nasty:
the Jehovah Witness rolled his *Watchtower* into a Chelsea
Brick and started knocking the shit out of that geezer
with a naff taste in brown and hair dripping Trojan 2000.
That was when I stopped laughing at ma own jokes
and listening to the afternoon play on Radio 4,
that was when despite being negritudous with sin,
I started throwing the stones, the Radio Times
and ma rather weighty tome of the complete works
of the Marquis De Sade.
And that was when they left, no real harm done,
promising to call back, perhaps some time next week
when I wouldn't be in.

Quiet Time Glanton

Spoilt for two kirks in a stone-clad
village nay bigger than Trumpton
or Camblewick Green
replete with its canny characters
and the occasional
relieved splutter of leaving traffic.

A choice of faiths
but finding more of a saving voice
in stray fractal bird-song
sometimes heard above
the omnipresent din of silence.

There's nothing metaphorical
in this place being cut-off,
its remoteness enforced by winter-weather,
some farmer, working the roads
with his third-hand tractor,
whistling 'there's no business
like snow business' –
at time and a half on a Sunday.

Probably the same gaje
herding his sheep through the village
primed with dampened pipe
and the dregs of slush shining off-white
in his copious bugger-straps
dripping from his ears,
eyes staring fixedly at the open gate
of his neighbour's field,
all that buckshee crazing ganning begging,
leaving the street littered with cac
and the chilling stink of life
coating country air.

Walk back with the dogs,
not finding a hare or rabbit
or summart for the pot,
exchange three phrases
with nearly neighbours,
your cloudy words
warming the brittle frost
of contented loneliness,
finding some crippled
sanctuary at last
to desecrate with futile praise.

Some

It felt good to be quite naked in the Balkans.
I was quite pleasantly surprised to have tunnelled so far,
perhaps, prison food did that for me.

That sun on my back was good
and the squelch of soft blood
between my toes was not unpleasant.

I met two people from Barnsley
who said that they came here every year
even under Tito or threat of redundancy.

The man, Neville, said I could borrow his hat.
His wife looked away at my perky erection,
and they knew a place where you could get
a traditional English Sunday Dinner reet cheap.

The sea was warm,
the beach was relatively un-spoilt
but I still found myself burrowing
back beneath the soil, breaking
my finger nails on old bones
and spent ammunition,
till I turned up at Calais
where the Wogs start getting grief
and found my passport photograph
looked nothing like me.

I claimed asylum.
I have been here ever since.
They say my condition is improving.
Today I was allowed a tennis ball
to bounce against the ward walls:
no one suspects anything yet, but
in another week I shall be through,
perhaps, maybe try Florida next year
if the exchange rate is half-ways decent.

Illiteracy

(For Geoff Hattersley, especially when clocking on)

At three everyone stopped for T,
which was a bit inconvenient
because it was Tuesday
and Tuesday's letter was Q.

The Foreman, up the arse
of management, sorting
out the plumbing of a time
and motion study, said, dinna
fuss, ambiguity of the sign, man!

It was a sign of the times
that we were all made redundant,
forced to queue in neat lines,
behind boxes that had letters
such as H and G or perhaps K,
and let me tell all the foremen
out there, you gotta stand in line
behind the right sign
however insignifying
you think you are.

It's good to Talk

she din't want to talk about the rapes
she din't want to talk about the incest
she din't want to talk about every time
I raised ma voice, she shook, thinking
I'd kick her teeth out, like the bloke
afore, and afore that twat an' all
she din't want to talk about every time
I touched her she wanted to scream,
cun't tek luving mi no more
But that cup, that forgotten dirty mug,
left by the side of the bath, by Christ,
she wanted to talk about that
            not that we ever did

Giving It the Works

Sat up all night
adjusting my Hope
Charity Shop training bra,
filling off finger-ends,
trying to make
myself more attractive
when the results come
in, more job losses
at 'The Works' – getting
my dander up, walking
down Buckingham Ave,
waving my placard,
'Devolution for Scunthorpe',
trailing after tumbleweed
and the rush for 'Double
Your Money Bingo' –
after all, what metaphysical
advantages have I ever given
my home town, 'cept been
born there and thereafter
shortly leaving, never
returning save when
they set fire to my Grandfather
at the Crematorium or the
visiting of relatives at Christmas
or redundancy wakes, but anyway,
I've done my bit, stood in line
and counted masel' lucky to leave
in one piece: "Up the Iron!"
as Grandfather would say,
watching Scunthorpe United
lose at home against
the Variety Club second eleven;

aye, someone blew the furnace out
and to be honest, despite my
protest placard, I can't really care,
a good place to leave -
steel, rust and tumbleweed.

Me and Mr Gilles De Tourette

apologies to et al...

Only other lunatics are amusing,
when you're ticking, when you're f-ing
among the 9 pence tins of baked beans in Aldi
and the girls on the tills are creaming
with laughter, when you're tupping away
like merry hell stuttering bits of words
like some neurotic semi-automatic
it's time that you and Mr Gilles De
Tourette had a good chat about it.
Hiding ma haldol in ma bottom drawer
lying to the next girlfriend about
verbal indigestion, bloated with tics
like an ald sheep's carcess,
you can't help to find the joke
in the sudden jerk that spills
the contents of mind naked on the air
like a newly born bastard bairn,
some devil-spawned child,
possessed with all the words
you don't get in a childers'
beginners dictionary.
You confabulate wildly,
talk excitedly,
lie through clenched teeth
the words won't stop,
tick-tock goes the clock,
shit-cunt-fuck
the clatter of heels,
the slammed catch of a suitcase,
jerking bits of goodbye
to the screech of tyres,
wondering if it was something

I said in bed, belting the bollocks
out of the springs with whatever
springs to mind
and mind your language
your Ps and Qs and FYs
and how you doing
Mr Gilles De Tourette?
I'm getting better,
ma lunacy beings to amuse me.

Mi Mate

for Vic Allen who appreciates a choice word or three, almost
as much as me

he'd never laugh, but cachinnate
he'd never shit, but defecate
a wank was out of the question
committing the sin of onanism
into a hand-sewn silk foulard
some such hanky-panky anyway
he'd deny he had excessive verbal diarrhoea
profess instead lucubracious logorrhoea
when he died choking on someone
else's words, we as one, who were not his friends,
performed the parrot sketch on his grave,
euphemistically mourning him in death
as in life along with the decline in spoken English

11/09/00

moved to Amble today,
first impression: two shop-lifters
in *Quality Fare* successfully
making off with a frozen chicken
and a bottle of white wine respectively –
unsure as to whether I'm glad
or not to be here,
but at least its cheap.

Possession is Nine-tenths of the Exorcism

He'd say things like, "are you a man or mouse –
come on, squeak up!" and make his son laugh,
sometimes by twisting his arm behind his back
till the chortles came, in stitches again.
He'd say things like, "Hey, broken-nose, play the piano!"
The first time his father said that, his son didn't have
no broken nose, and screw the rule on a double-negative.
He'd say a lot, but his son never squealed on him.
His son would cry to the theme tune of the Archers
just for something to do waiting for his Airfix glue
to hold him together. What do you know,
at seventeen after several futile attempts
he managed to give his girlfriend her first orgasm,
he didn't know how to tell the dog, Butch, that he was
no longer his best friend. At eighteen despite been
on the dole he won an all expenses paid holiday
to Thailand, his folks said, "Don't waste brass on
buying us presents!" He didn't. They never spoke
to him again. It was one small mercy in his life.
He flit to a bed-sit paid forty-four pounds fifty pence
for the privilege of different folks kicking his door down
or him in all for a bit of scag-heroin or devilment.
He asked his landlord to up the rent, he didn't
want it to be just another low rent tragedy,
putting all his money in the gas-meter and drinking it.
We buried him, we stood by his graveside and said
goodbye, you should have heard his father cry,
we applauded the sentiment, even when he ruined the moment,
spinning a few gags about Hitler gassing yids, gips and fags,
some people obliviously pass through life allus seeing
the funny side of everything –
it's enough to make you weep.

Stevie Wilkinson's Dog

Stevie would push his grandmother
around in her wheelchair,
it looked hard graft,
him ten year old
and struggling to grow up,
walk up Kirkhill
and to hold his head up
when he passed the bus stop,
us laughing and baiting,
struggling to grow up,
roll spliffs, get into pubs,
each other bodies,
just up to nay good.

Stevie would push his
lame Lancashire Hot-Pot Hound
and Jack Russell cross
in his dad's wheelbarrow.
That dog needed exercise.
Stevie didn't. He was struggling still
and the piss he took was unforgivable,
but at least by that time
we could roll spliffs, get into pubs
and more often than not into
each others' bodies – these small
compensations of life.

Stevie: didn't see him for years.
I was away fucking up universities,
working on building sites and other
things dull and not worth writing about.

This isn't about me. It's about Stevie,
saw him again down Walmgate pushing
a pram, hopefully it was his bairn inside,
the mother nay where in sight. Ma girlfriend
had stolen the contents of ma wallet and jeans
for some heroin, she was still depressed
about the abortion, Stevie was still pushing
his pram up to the lights, opposite
Jimmy's fish-ole. That was the last I saw
of him, though I read in the paper
about him hanging himself
and I wonder now and then
when I see a dog in a wheelbarrow
or some bairn pushing a gran,
just who fuck pushed him?

The Accidental Tourist

for F. le gradh mor

You make love in a shambolic
Welsh castle to someone you love
and you love it.

You return, walking boots, map and compass,
you see the tourist information board
in both Welsh and English,
notice your younger self hard at it,
jealous voyeur, you map out the years
that flow from the dog-knotted silhouette,
you finally get the compass bearing on this,
even though you've lost the path, the plot,
and all you can remember is that line of R.S.
Thomas, there is no future in Wales,
and the buttocks stop moving at last,
some gasp of joyous exhaustion, Biblical cum
spilt on the ground, 'cos you forgot a condom
and nay one can tell you a thing about
how to get back, move forward or that
track down from the keep covered
in soft green pellets of sheep cac.

The Joke

fourteen oozing testosterone
wanking about being
seduced by an older woman

now knackered and knocking on a bit
hoping like hell to meet
someone slightly younger

as for my original older woman
she's older still and not enjoying it
sometimes I see her on a street
in York, shopping, and she don't meet my eye
and I wonder what she don't see

Turning the Tide

What can I say,
Druridge Bay practising
ma Wu style, trying
to keep ma mind mindless,
interrupted by C++ or C
variables every time I tried
to grasp the bird's tail,
seeing the tide turn, out
of the corner of ma eye,
seeing this aging nudist
stroll bollock-naked along
the strand and unable
to maintain stillness
even when the wee man
had waddled around
the headland, especially
half an hour later
when two policemen
stood on the sand-tops
watching, still as stone,
minds as blank
as new-born cheque-books,
watching the silence,
waves skilting on the shore,
and a naked invisible man
make his way in the world.

One's Dirty Public Washing

Once I put ma boot through
a laundrette's window.
The sign said, "NO TRAVELLERS".

The next day, a board was up.
On the board were these words:
"NO TRAVELLERS".

That night I belted the board
hard as I could and hurt ma foot,
limped back to ma gaff
waited till they put back the glass
which they never did.
It was that sort of neighbourhood:
the only ones to use the place
were Blacks, Micks and stray dogs.

I left the London, still limping,
and every cripple has their own
way of walking, and perhaps
some folk need bigger boards,
till the next krystalnacht calls.

Welding

I went to ma mate's wedding
in a dead man's suit.
It woh real quality,
everything hand-sewn,
good cloth and the pants
lined in case I shat masen.

I didn't. I got drunk.
I told ma mate's mum
that it was the best
welding I'd ever bin to,
and, by the way, for years
I'd carried a torch for her.
She said, don't be soft, lad,
took out her 2-frunt teeth
and mock-snogged me.
I think I liked it.

Her husband called me
a bounder. I woke up
underneath the chairs
at the Polish club,
sick on a dead man's suit,
cringing for an open-cast
mine to swallow me,
but at least I didn't shit masel',
for that I am deeply grateful, amen.

Cunnilinguistics

What do cunts want?
In ma experience
they want you to say couldn't instead,
but I cun't do it.

They mek me sick
the way they tek the piss
out of the underclass
for saying fuck
every other word.

Av' they tried it?
Can they do it?
I fucking tried fucking it
fucking once fucking hard
fucking thing fucking to
fucking do.

What do cunts want?
They want to try
getting fucked around,
then we'll hear how
eloquent they really sound.

Weather Girls

It was raining again in Amble,
not that that mattered,
there was every girl
I'd ever done wrong to
crammed tight in ma room.

I didn't hear them come in,
but I still felt bad about it;
women everywhere, stacked
like skeletons in ma cupboard;
there was even Emma squat
in ma sock drawer –
how the heck they managed that
I just don't know: Mrs O'Flaherty
didn't know and her husband's
a plumber, so there you go.

It was bad in there,
it smelt of bruised promises,
out of date bad faith,
and love that had gone off
and died like something left
in the fridge for a rainy day.

'This really is paranoia,' I said,
just to be moving ma lips.
When Jane with a 'why' said,
'Bloody egomanic - it is just us,
and it's a small room,
not so chuffing many, charva,
the rest of the world don't give
two fucks about you.'

I wasn't sure.
Pushing past a girl
that I still loved I made it
to the window and checked
on the weather.
It was chocker out there,
bastards were queuing already,
worse than the petrol shortage,
worse than the miner's strike –
what it is to be
unpopular.

Fudging it

They were discussing the Euro,
how undervalued it was,
whether it was worth
buying cheap and selling dear,
whether it was worth entering
or not, would it too unstable,
would it damage the domestic economy,
was it the future,
was it the way to go –
sorry I've forgot the question marks:
?????????
it was that sort of party.

She said she wasn't in love with me,
which was understandable,
and had I tried the olives stuffed
with almonds, which I hadn't:
the debate about the Euro
hetting up, folk were hedging
their bets.

She got drunk. Nearly as
drunk as me, deliriously celebrating,
having found those fabled olives -
stupendous.

In the kitchen washing out
ashtrays, spittoons and ma
rather limited vocabulary, she
confessed to never having experienced
rimming before.

There was a granny flat in the garret,
so after borrowing a toothbrush,
then brushing ma tongue I obliged.
Afterwards, she was interested in perhaps
trying it on a regular basis,
other activities too, though
she wasn't in love, perhaps
I could manage a little gentle
buggery, as she'd never tried that
either. I checked someone else's
electronic diary, they'd been a movement
in the price of the Euro against
a basket of other currencies,
including the Yam Balaat of Outer Mongolia.
I had a re-start interview, the dentist,
an appointment with a housing association,
but no gentle buggery pencilled in.
Tuesday, we agreed on Tuesday afternoons
after the Archers repeat, she didn't kiss me
goodbye, specks of saliva, shit and possible
salmonella bacteria was a little
off-putting, but we'd do lunch
and things were looking
up, later in the week,
despite fluctuations in the Euro.

Famished

After enduring all those barren years of Tory misrule
I turn the telly on by mistake
to get turned on by Nigella Lawson
eating of, all things, luxury Yorkshire Pudding –
now that, really takes the biscuit.

Tolstoy on a Horse
Peter Knaggs

Contents

Part One: HU5

Part Two: An Astronaut Lands in Chants Ave

Part Three: Verisimilitude

Part One: HU5

The Door Bell Is Ringing

Don't think of his brains
dashed out by half bricks,
four finger-shaped bruises
fruiting on the upper arm,
a wagless tongue lolled
like a drunk horse,
a blue face, or a boot lace
drawn around the neck.
Don't think about
his favourite superman
T shirt disturbed,
or his tiny fractured finger
poking out like a twig
from a shallow covering,
or the police Alsation
sniffing in the brambles,
barking at the nettles,
and four policemen running
over, as slow as they can.

A Man In Chanterlands Avenue Slices An Onion

A size enough to hold in the hand,
to sit there nice, the fingers to shape
round it, like a bowler measuring
a yorker, he holds the weight of it,

of hearing it on the radio, Keegan
the little boy left in the pushchair
outside *Faxons,* onion skin stretched
old suitcase tan, bright as linoleum,

Keegan missing, his mother hysterical.
He heard about it first on the radio
at work, and a row of tiny black
falling stars are pricking the root.

Equidistant thin wood lines under-wire
the papery wrapping, imagine it
your boy, measured as hand-made sweets,
smooth as chestnut, hard as turnip.

He pulls a knife across the onion top,
tipped by a scrunch of old document,
dry as dead flowers. On the front page
of *The Hull Daily Mail* was a photo

of the missing toddler and a headline,
before the onion is sliced it's gentle
assault on the nose no more
than cricket match teas, a jar lid,

your fingers the day after cooking,
"HULL BOY KEEGAN AGE 3 GOES MISSING
  WHILE MOTHER GOES SHOPPING,"
    the onion skin, fissured, split,

reveals it's sallow under-layer
bursting out of it's shirt.

Richard To The Till, Please

They usually bawl at first,
Richard to the till please.
He's a miserable bastard,
could scowl for England.

Today , Richard gets stuck
in her throat, she's thinking
about Keegan, poor Keegan,
all our thoughts are with Keegan

and his poor mother. At school,
at all the schools in Hull
the headmistresses and headmasters
ask their children to say a prayer,

for the missing little boy Keegan,
and it catches us all in the throat
and were all playing with our eyes
with a bent finger. With some

it's more uncontrollable than others,
like the girl in *Faxons,* stooping
over the microphone, Richard,
she needs to be off the shop floor,
Richard to the till, please.

Tolstoy On A Horse

not finding his way to the *Dundee Chippy*,
on a hunched shoulders of a night
and a bag of chips nowadays
is not really a bag of chips in my book

when it's a polystyrene carton.
But you would hardly say,
'*A polystyrene carton of chips,*
wrapped, sports pages please luv,"
jostle hot potato around your tongue,
under the pin holes of the stars,
the fat arse of the moon,
in goat beard socks, in elk-
skin boots, in wolf hide chaps.

Only Tolstoy, the fat jockey
splays a fine black stallion,
runs chewed fingers through his beard,
clambers off, fastens his horse
to the leaky drainpipe, jams

2 bike lamps in his backside pockets,
chucks the saddle over his arm,
contemplating sallow potatoes,
misinterpreting, one of each and chips
twice, missing the sound of burlaki,
birch bark soles softly thumping
the sunlit duckboard in summer
or on a hunched shoulders of a night,
Russian mud, the consistency of dough.

Tolstoy Sits Down To Watch Blind Date

Tolstoy asked, '*What do people do round here*
on a Saturday night?' I yawned out,
'*We're usually knackered, so we watch a bit of telly.*'
His lemon wedge eyebrows arched quizzically.
He opened out the flats of his palms,
'*You go to a bookshop for the day, Peter.*'
I nearly answer, "*But,*" but he prods the air
with a condyled finger, '*does this programme,*
Blind Date, *give or take from life experience?*'
I toe my wife's line, '*It's escapism.*'
Me, the man with no sense of humour,
later we spin large measures of vodka.
Tolstoy leans closer, "*This* Blind Date *Peter,*
It makes time pass, but puts it to no use, no?"

Tolstoy In The Bathroom

Tolstoy loves the bathroom,
locks himself in whole mornings,
his muffled baritone of Russian song
filling our home, as Tolstoy empties
half a bottle of shampoo in one go,
smears his armpits and chest
with massive dollops of strawberry
shower gel, burns all the aromatherapy oils
at once and a whole packs of joss sticks, scrubs
his fat tummy with a long-handled bath-brush
while tackling his shoulder with the loofah.
His footprints splatter the bath-mat,
all the brighter for the talcum powder
outline and although he doesn't shave,
he sprinkles aftershave on his shirts,
billows himself in a cloud of *Java*,
three toothbrushes now in the bathroom.
Toothpaste, he eats it we think.
He loves the smell of himself
asks us to breathe it.

In Praise Of Tin Openers

Like legs of scissors
or handles of clippers,
a butterfly key
now a hard block of plastic,
a cog and a circular blade
to hook on the lip,
to puncture and pierce the rim,
to roll around clockwise,
a scooting incision
at the twist and wheel
of thumb and first finger.

Your only trustworthy utensil
west side of the kitchen-
drawer, I'm telling you boy
for bareknuckled wing-nut
spinning he's your man,
the only apparatus
for unlocking
your aluminium exit,
not roughshod or jerky,
jagged or bodged,
no dastardly tricks,
flicking back like a pike,
splattering beans,
or nicking your finger.

No Jack of all trades
this mans a specialist,
a tin cutting champion,
a kitchen drawer yardstick.
Shove your melon-baller,
apple corer, fondue kit,
your pizza cutting poncey

wedding gift gadgets.
Stick your waste of spacers,
kitchen drawer clutterers.
No *Teflon* midnight runner
or a fad that changes overnight
or breaks in the night,
not the latest newfangled
gizmo, got-to-have gimmick
from *Lakeland Plastics,*
give me a man I can trust
to open my soup
and call him Elvis.

Poem On Toenails And Vacuum Cleaners

Lashed like Gulliver in Lilliput,
a toenail hooked by nylon carpet
fibre, a curling crescent snagged down,
opaque bone, a slither of human tusk.

Mine? My wife's? Mister House's?
Mr House's budgie's? A Halloween remnant,
my wife won't touch it, on the grounds
of a lack in the nail varnish department.

Or is it a fingernail bitten to the quick.
Have the clippers clipped it,
firing it off in a southwest direction,
an ensuing search proving fruitless?

Or maybe chewed off during a semi-final
and spat across the room, or peeled back
from the toe by a thumb and a finger.
I first noticed it months ago.

Time to wheel the vacuum out
from the cupboard under the stairs,
unwind the hoop of electrical cord,
I don't mind so much vacuuming myself

but hate the noise of other people
doing it. Attacking the brittle slither
of bony carpet gripping critter,
I run the *Hoover* back and forth,

nail suctioned up to the mouth-part.
Bounce. Clawed back by the octopus-
like tentacles of carpet fibre,
tightening their grip, tightening their knit.

A Woman On Chanterlands Avenue
Peels a Potato

The blade transmits a hushed insect sound,
perhaps a cricket signalling, or frost
or snow being scraped and the wan eye
opens up, sallow. As the peeler wheels

the island grows bigger, the sea decreases.
When she heard, the toddlers abduction had been
on her street, she spat out her mouthful

of sandwich, after the interminable ring
of the phone, her heart nearly burst,
to hear her mother coo at the other end.

The bitten sandwich stayed on the table
with the *Twix* wrappers, today's papers
and yogurt pots. She went back to work
thinking only   thank God.

He toddles in with paper and crayon.
Happy he lays on the floor. He's drawing
her in the kitchen, illustrating
mummy at the window, peeling a potato

weathered as a worker with no choice
but to be out in the sun all day, cut
and gashed, nicked and bitten, rashed
with flecks, a map of the Scottish Islands

or dish-stuck *Alpen.* Wasn't breakfast an age
before Debbie blabbered out the radio news,
'*A boy has gone missing on Chanterlands Avenue,*'
and put her innards through the mangle.

Coat-colour of dusty honey or murky syrup,
the island dilates, sailing the peeler
until there's no sea left, just the centre.

The fodder crop, osculant to her palm
feels warmer and wetter and clammy.
The curls of potato peel mooch in the sink.
She went to school with her mum, poor thing.

Towel

Let me think. If I had to be one,
it would have to be a big blue beach towel,
sporting a crab, a seahorse, a whale,
an octopus and a fish, of unknown species.

A child's drawing of a fish, mouth triangle,
maybe once a year lugged out,
shaken and spread by an Italian pool
on a sun-bed for a beautiful girl

lazed in my blue cotton, in her swim suit.
Sun bathing her golden as honey on toast.
My threads coughing up brine, sandy,
with an aftertaste of factor eight.

Snug on my cozy airing cupboard shelf,
the other towels could moan at the boring view
of toothbrushes, toothpaste, bathroom wall.

I'd yawn, hibernating for the winter,
dreaming of holidays, of my sunbather.

A Question Of Gravity

OK Newton
with your laws of motion and gravitation,
did you ever work out
how these rules apply to the bedroom?

Solve this conundrum
with your ratios, grades, angles and heights
using a protractor, a compass,
your theories and laws of physics and maths.

Take my bed
layered two cotton sheets, an old wool blanket,
a bedspread, a quilt,
when it's cold a blue sleeping bag, unzipped.

When I tug the bedspread
quilt, blanket sheet and sleeping bag, unzipped,
is it the wind-stream
or drag-force countersinking the weight,

or a pivot which tips
her at a determinable point, measured
in Kilo-joules, Kilo-Newtons,
iotas, millimetres or a kelvin of heat?

How does the speed
I pull the bedding towards me remain constant
to the speed she shuffles
across to a micro-millimetre per second?

At the slightest re-adjustment
calibrated in the momentum of the bedding
my wife retains
the equilibrium of a bubble in the spirit level.

Stop-watched by quartz
her timing is precise. Does her abdomen
have a magnetic pull,
a pole attracted by Celsius, or Fahrenheit?

At the time
to turn out the light, crisply tucked in,
the stripes of the bedspread
are aligned to the frame of the bed.

Two hours later I wake,
sheet, blanket, blue sleeping bag, unzipped
have transported
and are residing in my wife's direction

Leaving my knees bare
and toes exposed Isaac. Computate this
nocturnal subtraction,
teach me the theory of eiderdown juxtaposition.

Yet most amazing of all
Newton, puzzle me this biological feat,
the whole time
my wife remains fast asleep.

A Question Of Seasons

and Newton while I'm here
there's another thing,
how do I tell when winter
is turning to spring?

The radius of the moon
in an algebraic equation
involving two abuci
and a navigators sextant,
the length of a shadow
on the sundial
divided by the time
of a solar eclipse?

No. I can calculate
this one using my head,
my wife stops wearing
her socks in bed.

Sock

If I had to be one
it would have to be a football sock
of a striker or a high scoring winger,
size ten, hundred percent nylon,
dressing the battered shin pad
of a higher calibre of player,
a man of ability, pushing promotion,
laundered by older cheerful ladies,
with bodies made for cuddling,
generous with their softener.

Pegged on the washing line
what stories we'd share
of leg-breaking tackles,
Stapleton chips and Cantona tricks,
school boy errors, point blank misses,
our crazy keeper my main man
of the match award competition,
with oh so funny impersonations,
'*You cannae dae that at this level*
and expect tae get away wi it.'

My worst mare, bottom of the kitbag,
sick as a parrot, suffocating under
a centre-half's armpit.
When I get older I wouldn't mind
too much an early bath now and then,
to be lost for a while, under the bed,
not missed, found in time for a testimonial,
reunited with the kiss of a parted friend.
For my man his lucky shooting socks
would nab a belter of a hatrick,
back to the drawer, to the banter
with his work socks, walking socks,

teasing the new uns like debutantes
on the slim chance of a spin
with her knickers, reminiscing
on the kit women, ironing us,
twinning us up and cuffing us,
on match days feeling sick,
topping the laundered, laid out pile,
eyes stealing up the white ceramic
and that pre-kick off anticipation
you wouldn't swap for anything,
that twist in the stomach, in the sole.

Nuptial Flight

It's a balmy day,
I'm trying to read,
'The Floating Egg,'
but lose my way
every three pages.
My concentration
can't even extend
to an argument,
our bickering
petering out.

I lug the deck-chair
out into the garden,
it's teeming
with big fat ants
and winged ants.

I read less than a page
of, 'The Floating Egg.'
My calf starts itching.
I go in and shut the door.
My wife asks me crossly
why I've shut the door.

The Myrmecologist

i) I'm in the garden drinking tea
   watching the ants, I am eating
   the last piece of lemon slice.
   Crusts of icing have stuck to
   the crenulations on the sides
   of *Mr. Kipling's* plastic casing.
   Ants eat sugar, so I chuck it
   down to them. Annabel gets moody,
   she wanted those bits.

ii) All worker ants are female,
    at first they ignore
    the icing sugar debris,
    then one or two workers
    clamber on, filling up
    their mandibular glands,
    then scurry to the nest.
    At the nest they dance,
    to cause excitement.
    Five minutes later
    a troop of rusty red
    slightly larger ants
    are all over the place.

Take That You Fucker

Elbow guarding my dressing gown, swathing
an *Evening Press,* rolled up, precarious on
the frame of our bed, I am shooing a wasp,

but the

ceiling

is too

high, the

window

is too far

ahead,

not open

enough,

the wazzie

won't dip,

headbutt,

headbutt,

headbutt

the pane.

A fisted swat, a tennis swerve motion, the wasp
circling our light fitting. I know he's zippy,
got some sting in that tail and me, only in my

dressing gown. I blast aftershave. I miss. I coax,
'Please escape mister wasp, I'll waft you in the right
direction, go home.' I teeter on the bed-frame,

over-reach
exposing
a second
of thigh.
I try to
bat the
window
wider
open
it won't
budge
white
emulsion
dried
on the

sash-rope. I retreat into the sinking mattress, grasping
my tartan dressing gown, fuckin wasp whizzing just out
of reach. Back down, headbutt, headbutt, headbutt
memory lapse, headbutt, the pane. Gottyer. Nuzzling
the gap between the windows. I swoop for the blue chair,
jump on it, spray enough *Boss* to marmalyse the bastard.

Will it though? Will the spores weigh on his wings,
Send his navigation system haywire? It could do. He is
                                        doddering,
                              my breath
                          judders
                      with the
                    window
              I'm heaving
          down,
            down,
        so there's
      just
        enough
      room
      to thrust
    in the
    Press.
      Prod
    prod,
  prod.
He's dead
and my dressing gown falls open to the world.
No one was there to see me, at that glorious moment.

Strawberry

Pick me from my punnet.
Slice me clean in half.
Douse me, drench me,
quench your thirst,
pluck my leafy crown.
See me stubbly, dimpled,
wet paint bright
until white cream holds me
cold and tight.

Wait for my fruitiness to burst
from my candy-floss heart,
fizzing a fountain of lemonade,
zinging down your throat,
swimming butterfly stroke,
kicking your tastebuds gently,
snowboarding your tongue
in my flavoursome quest.

Fresh cool and counting
in my punnet corner, excited
by each swing of the hinge,
sideways glances to the cream.
Are you ready for me yet?
We were made for each other.

Philip My Extraordinary Fridge

Philip, sentry to one inch of tahini
and a jar of cocktail cherries,

like an armchair gracing the room with your hum
and frozen food rules for a phaze,
fish-fingers, burgers and chips in the freezer,
dollopped with fridge-cooled fresh mayonnaise.

Fridgy has his demands, a clean now and then.
A plug feeds his small appetite.
Ice lips the freezer, requesting defrosting,
so we defrost Philip overnight,

while he rinses the kitchen in fridge-
light, *Ribena* props open the door.
Like a puppy he leaks all over the lino,
so the mop gets to cuddle the floor.

When the motor cuts in with it's jiddery jig,
I believe a man's best friend is his fridge.
He knows his job, needs not to be told
the importance of keeping that four-pack cold.

November, I painted his rust spots up,
motor slowing, I strolled around pretending
not to notice his lungs were collapsing,
sealant splitting, fridgy was shivering

and where there was a relaxing hum,
he jerks like a car without enough choke.
He chokes like a miner minus his ale.
How do I nurse him through his old age?

My index finger slips down *Yellow Pages*.
I stroke my chin over which engineer
has the friendlier name, financial criteria
low down on my list of things to consider.

To lighten his load, to help with his wheeze,
we get in a freezer, repair bills rise.
So I pay in cash and bin the receipts.
The life of a fridge boils down to this.

Knackers yard, scrap man are not allowed
to be mentioned. For electrical goods
whisper, kitchen heaven. We thrash out
the details late into the night,

polishing off a bottle of old single malt,
and when they came to take old fridgy away,
I was at work, not dwelling upon it.

Noah and Swim

The goldfish are separate sides
of the tank, like petulant lovers.
Noah might have been biting Swim's tail.
I'd never know. I can't talk to them.
I just watch them mouth, O, O, O.

A Glass Of Water For The New Millennium

Over to the kitchen sink by the window.
A gut full of bad champagne, an empty flute
in my hand, my wife in bed, about to follow,
but before I put my head down on the pillow

I put the flute on the draining board.
I want something before I go to bed.
The fireworks are dead, bread-sticks and dips
half finished, in the bread-bin, in the fridge.

We've toasted the new millennium in.
I'm stood with my hands on the aluminium
rim of the sink. I take myself a glass
move it under the spout and turn on the tap.

Part Two: An Astronaut Lands in Chants Ave

An Astronaut Lands in Chants Ave

The idea appealed to me,
like the thought of a falling star
stabbing the roof, it sitting there,
emitting an odour of sulphur,
tin foil next to the chimney, bending
the T.V. aerial and spitting out
the blackhead of the satellite dish.
All the people on Chants Ave
pointing at it and going on about
the rumour of a rocket in the corner
of Western Cemetery, a prank,
a stunt or as real as the astronaut
at the student's three doors down.
They took him to *Spiders* nightclub
and he had trouble separating
those new 5ps with his space-gloves.
'*Hull's brilliant,*' he beamed,
or when asked, *having a good time?*
He gave the thumbs up sign.

Secretary of Space

Fighter craft pilot
all in one outfit,
loose off the bone
like the hide of a rhino,
all zips and velcro
and detachable pockets
for pens and notebooks,
somewhere between
a deep sea diver
and a formula one driver,
un-sponsored, his helmet
stuck on like a nose cone
or a deodorant top,
the rim screwed into place
and tightened up
with a jubilee clip,
a container strapped
to his back
like a council worker
spraying weed-killer
and a climber's harness
strung like a nappy,
hitched up and hooked up
with caribenas and buckles,
gloved up knuckles
and little thermometer tubes
hooped to his arms,
a mini life-jacket necklace
and three inches below
the belly button line
a strap clunked in
to a seat belt retainer,
on the left protruding
a glass tube not dissimilar
to those found in

the earliest televisions,
right side an object
resembling a hose-pipe
stuck out with a connection nut
like the hot water lead
behind a washing machine,
but is probably a critical
respiratory instrument.

Lorra Lorra Lorraine

Although Anthony had told me about
often seeing her at the *Dundee Chippy,*
absolutely gorgeous he said she were.
Despite being with my wife
that first time I saw her,
I couldn't take my eyes off her.
It was on Westbourne Avenue,
about midway down, near the fountain
with the curly-haired angel-man
and the giant green haddock.
Notwithstanding it being a fountain,
I'd never seen the water pouring,
not a puny drip of drizzle or gozz
spouting from any of their sculpted lips.
Maybe the council never switched it on.
She was in a grey cotton top,
one of those with a drawstring hood,
with the emblem of three giant letters.
Whereas Anthony said she was beautiful,
I never thought that she was, nonetheless
insofar as not being able to keep my eyes
off her, I was being extremely rude.
She had a curious condition, which meant
that she couldn't stop brushing her hair.
She radiated happy un-embarrassment,
her un-rebuking eyes held high, just proud
of stroke after stroke and her scuttling
as if late, brushstroke after brushstroke
curling it in at the fringe at each fall
of her trainer, on the damp pavement
that day I first saw her.

Tolstoy Hears About The Price Of Cucumber

He puts his washing out from middle.
I start from left I do, unless
it's raining and it often is
nowadays, but if summat's needed
I chuck it in't tumble drier.
can't imagine life withoout it,
then I hang it on clothes horse
in't front room. Jessica,
Jessica says you can roast potatoes
in twenty minutes. As if.
Roast potatoes in twenty minutes,
my foot. She said she cut em up small.
They'd have to be bloody small n'all.
Socks, I don't know, is it me?
Do I walk further, or don't socks last long
these days? Always wearing out.
I bought this pair just last month,
me toes burst through already
and I don't have sharp toenails,
no, I clip them quite often, anyhow
I an't got all day to stand here gassing
and there's nothing much on telly
nowadays and that's another thing...

Hull Girl On Find A Mate

Hello contestant number 3,
What's your name?
The girl who can't stop
brushing her hair
keeps brushing her hair.
Audience, I want you to meet Lorraine.
Lorraine comes from Hull.
Well I suppose someone has to.
The cue card man lifts a cue card,

  'Hysterical laughter.'

Now Lorraine you're a student.
Worrayestudyin luv?
The girl who can't stop
brushing her hair
keeps brushing her hair.
Now Lorraine's studying cod.
Uncontrollable laughter.
Only codding.
Now Lorraine, you don't like
application forms do you?
Because when your given one,
you have to fillet in.
Cue the cue card man,

  'Laugh as if a joke
    has never been so funny, ever.'

Celia Hilarious is off again,
I hear you're a big D-ream fan,
that your particular fave is,
'Things Can Only Get Battered.'

The girl who can't stop
brushing her hair
keeps brushing her hair.
Hull though, it's a lovely place.
The audience howl like demented donkeys.
No seriously, I went there once, Bought
a box of fishcakes. They were nice.
Hull it's easy to find like,
take a bus to the end of the world,
at the terminal, jump off.
The studio audience laugh.
Celia Hilarious is shaking her head,
Right we'll do that last bit again,
Okay audience, you didn't laugh enough.
The cue card man picks a different card.

Lorraine's Reaction To Not Being Picked

Kevin, you turned down Lorraine
from Hull. How could you?
Come in number 3.
The girl who can't stop brushing
her hair stays sat on her stool.
She keeps brushing her hair.
There is no change of pace.

Osram, Sony, Lena Zavaroni

The smear of brown pickle has dried
like a thumbprint to the plate.
Two inches of tea remain cold,
painting a ring around the mug radius.
Must have a word in his shell-like.
I drop into the armchair, haul
the paper squeezed under my backside,
no news in Hull. Then my eyes
are pulled to an article on the right.

I tip my head back. I'm examining
the ceiling, then reading the light bulb.
Osram, was there a fella called *Osram?*
Osram the light bulb man, or *Sony?*
Mister *Sony,* some branding that.
Osram, maybe he missed his opportunity.

The water works into the radiator.
It's innards creak that metallic eking.
Lena Zavaroni with only £40 a week
for food and heating, alone in a flat,
a black and white pic of her draggled perm.
She is no longer with us, the singer
who shot to fame on *Opportunity Knocks.*

Dear Jack,
How are the fish?

Walloping up the M1
from the North
on bald tyres,
catch it butterfingers,
a dandelion clock.
It stops, a train, shrieking,
listen to that
scale, that won't budge
off the fish-knife
running under
a cold water tap.
Tune in to a battered wireless,
a busted up and knotted
elastic band holding it
together. Poetry you see
is cushty,
Five fish rammed
into an electric kettle,
It gets in your hair
like a wasp or oil
on the release button
of an old pram wheel.
Zooming like ants,
from the beautiful north.
Stop staring at it bastard.
Is thee pegging cogs
at Sue Smith's white sheets?
It'll break your fingers
like a concrete block
dropped on a *Saab*
from the foot-bridge
at the underpass.
Poetry, it's the spaghetti

in a western, spitting
your grandad's punched out teeth
into the mashed potato.
It's got a big red cock
like a dog
that's just had
a fuckin good shag.
Pick a number, any number,
seventy seven,
asserting it's scruffy
white paint identity
over a shiny grey wheelie bin.
It carries home that sharp sound
of a can of *Tango*
being snapped open.
It's shot and knotted
like 2 ½ lb *Bayer Perlon*,
caught in Monks Hood,
to strangle swans.
Push it. It's a knife point
forced at Sotheby's throat.
It runs like fingers
over the elastic battlement
impressed in the skin,
near the thigh bone,
that you might carp-kiss,
but you won't.
You can't leave it alone.
So keep it under your noodle,
your bonnet, your hood.
Poetry is the new feng-shui.
Poetry is the new cod.

Boff

We all heard it.
Everyone turned.
He farted
in a spacesuit.
Only he smelt it.

Tolstoy Catches Up On The Gossip

Not that I've ever really heard one,
but you can imagine the sound
would take you back in time,
an old gramophone record
wheeling out of it's horn,
sound-tracking a different age.
My mouth turned down like a trout
at the sink at the window,
his bulldozer bucket of a cake-hole
booming like a tenor with laughter.
I can't help laughing at Tolstoy,
in the yard with the scissors,
cutting some mint, Christine's
head bobbing over the garden fence.
I don't know if he knows where L.A. is.
Bringing a soap sudded mug to rest
on the draining board, I'm drumming
up explanations of cartoons, Hollywood,
and it's good that Christine's son
is the new Freddy Flintstone.

But when Tolstoy comes in, he doesn't ask.

Capes, MacGowan, Sheene, Whiteside, Bristow, Flynn

If I could have a one to one
it would have to be with John.
We'd go the *Polar Bear*
and ask the barmaid to top up
the heads on our pints.
I'd ask him about business,
about Ludvik, when he's going
to come over for the dog racing.

If I could have a one to one
tt would have to be with my mate John.
Famous people don't know you
like your friends. I could tell
him about this unbridled summer,
how it's pulling so fast
I want to tether it back
like a gypsies horse. Press pause
on this tape, stop and yawn,
or land like a bee and harvest
pollen like thoughts on my nose.
But time keeps springing towards
a finishing tape, like a retriever
bounding after a tennis ball
thrown by it's owner.

I'd tell John how the whole summer
my heads felt hungover,
my limbs ache in a hundred places,
my muscles, a fisherman's catapult
pulled, the year yet to explode,
to kick in or kick-start
like a motorbike displaced like
the time, the football season
booting off earlier than early,

in the centre-circle of summer.
It's just not right, August,
my wife tucked up upstairs
with a hot water bottle.
I'm squinting through the keyhole,
coterminous, on the perimeter,
ankles in the starting blocks
with only the difficult task
of keeping balance.
Take last Monday at the bank machine,
inserting my *Barclaycard,*
clear forgetting my number.
For all the world stumped,
an 11 plus student gnawing
a pencil at the easiest question,
my PIN number AWOL, on leave,
is it gormless me, or is something
of this summer not in the air
like pollution, an aspect unborn
that I can't put my finger on?

Last Will And Testament

Please don't leave the world
with nothing to remember me by.
I'm not after a brief small slab
with a holey tub in a crematorium,
or even something as normal
as a gravestone. A Statue.
That's more my cup of char.
Take an old giant oak would you,
to carve an angel to look after me?
Or better still get to grips
with a tomahawk and chisel, set about
a twelve foot tall totem pole,
complete with grimacing beaks.
Then again, get your sewing kit out,
to embark on a three year project
of my life story, embroidering parts
in brighter colours, harder stitches.
I want you to do something for the world
to keep as a memory, that's not easy,
like the Bayeaux Tapestry.
LFO to collaborate with *Utah Saints*
on a dance remix of a tribute
to me, and there has to be a bit
that goes, '*Utah Saints, Utah Saints,*
U U U U U Utah Saints.
In my obituary don't slouch
with that pen. Give me rhythm
and a certain dexterity of syntax,
to go down in the library of elegy.
At my funeral, cry as if it's the end
of the world. To cope at my wake,
knock back a river of whisky.
Please won't you do this for me,
and say the nicest things about myself
and about me.

Not Including A Pigeon

I couldn't give a toss Tolstoy.
That horse is not coming
into our house.

For a start it won't fit,
second Mr. House says
were not allowed pets.

Tether it up in't yard.
Look here's a few quid,
buy a bunch of bike locks.

Kids round here nick anything
including horse legs.

Tolstoy Blattering On About Deodorant

My ankle goes topsy-turvy, paddling a foothold
I tumble down a cleave in the escarpment.
Captured and brabbled, I'm bound, rendered
a prisoner. Vines clamp tight my fat wrists.
The sentries march me to a camp in the slade,
.inhabited by only embronzed Amozonian women,
with globous breasts

                              disaster
a two-headed monster attacks the camp.
Tall as a big house , I keep an eyeball
on his cuspids as my tattered captors
scatter like pigeons. Tolstoy the brave
retains courage, wit, genius enough to grab
a furry breast strap, a festinate sling.
I load a rock missile and whirl my arm
threaded with hope. I slay the monster.
They trophy the carcass. I am king Tolstoy.
Because I purchased a can of *Lynx,*
and squirted deodorant on my arm pits,
I am witness to hundreds of fantastic young
Amazonian tits, bouncing, dancing, jiggling
and jouncing and jiggling and jiggling.

The Visitors

Astronaut, we're here.
Are you coming out?
We know you're in there.

Come on outside.
We just want to talk.
Are you coming out?

Astronaut, we're here.
We're not going anywhere
until you come out.

We know you can hear us.
We know you're in there.
Remember. We were here.

Fish

Goldfish, two by two
Noah and Swim circle up
and down in blue.

Kebab Meat (Part One)

'*The Avenue,*' leaks cornflake drunks
pours them into a bowl, *Italiano's,*
fingerprints vanish an impression
into the aluminium fridge-casing.
Dartboard blurts,
                    '*I want Donna in a kebab,*
roll that sexy chick in a pitta bread,
with salad, chilli sauce and yogurt.'
Pepperoni flavoured dog food swirls
With wafts of burnt flour. Perfect,
for soaking up cheap *Spiders* lager.
Elvis slams both palms on the counter,
'*Gimme an I'm ace at shagging-*
I've got a big cock and I'm-
a fuckin ard twat kebab. Please'

'*Eh Astro, you having a doner?*'
Astro turns his space-gloved thumb,
signals negative. '*Come on Astro.*
You gotta eat. I ain't seen you eat.
We ain't seen you eat nothing, ever.'
'*Two small doners,*' Ponytail nods.
Tolstoy trots by, on a horse,
a traffic cone planted on his bonce.
Dandling from the horses arse, a bike light.
The astronaut waves, Dartboard waves
and Elvis, the blokes behind the counter wave.
Tolstoy clops past. '*Las polabras des amore,*
let me eer the wuds ov lov,'
the kebabman sings, to a tinny radio.

Kebab Meat (Part Two)

Dartboard's gonna chunder
unless he can drink his sen back sober,
needs to do a nash back to their house.
'*No Astronauts in Hull,*' spraycanned
in silver across the *Smartie* yellow door,

still wet, still that *Airfix* glue,
that industrial workshop smell,
it's nice but for the acrid stink of racism,
undersigned BNP, they're coming
and that was *Queen* and *Freddy Mercury*.

Dartboard, Elvis and Astro braced
at the curb, tip back their coffee-pot-
lid-heads, claw up and lower
ribbons of lamb, drunk-hungry jowls

salivating as their incisors attack.
The throat igniting chilli-red sauce
is treated by cold sour yogurt.
Shredded watery iceberg lettuce
is already soggying the wrapping.

As joyriders, taxis and late nighters
top up the carbon monoxide,
Elvis licks a trickle of chilli sauce
& yogurt mix leaking down his wrist.

Dartboard's got an NVQ in marketing,
'*Mmmm yummy kebab meat, nutritious,
healthy, tasty and good for vegetarians.*'
His head is swaying. His pitta bread shapes
itself into doughy lips, emits a dirty burp.

Growls at him, '*Shut the fuck up Dave.*'
Heeling on the curb of Chants Ave,
they jam kebab into their drunken gobs,
except Astro who doesn't eat his.
He just stands their and holds it
like a space-poet holding an open book.

As The Hands Go Up, The Teacher Matches Those Of A Similar Height.

White collars and smaller sized black ties,
four infant shoulders a prop for the weight
of the funeral procession on Chanterlands Avenue.
The brevity of their paces inducing
a failure of terms to bewilderingly approach.
It's down to Jordan's teacher to, *please ask
Keegan's brothers class for volunteers
to be the pallbearers for Jordan's brother,*
the toddler Keegan who disappeared
from *Faxon's* forecourt, flower smothered
with the message, all we have are cards,
and although the coffin is not to heavy,
it pushes an impression into the velvet collar.

Poem Concerning The Factors Interfering With The Chance And Possibility Of Bus Drivers Meeting Their Schedule

Or so the bus window fogs up, you arch
your hand and smear a patch of window clear.
Framed by condensation you see a *Peugot* wing
punched in and indicator plastic, scattered

fed to the birds like broken biscuit now.
And whenever it rains will it bring to mind
passengers queued to a wide-screen, gormless
at their own windscreen show, missing Cilla,

or the wide arse of the paramedic,
each time wet gears shift down along Spring Bank,
a mucky green stretcher being loaded,
or rain like gristle and a police car on the corner.

The girl with the curious condition
which meant she couldn't stop brushing her hair
has stopped. No one retrieves the still hairbrush.
Through the mist it sits, sideways to the road

rainy and irretrievably out of reach.

Car Park Accident Face

Tolstoy's not looking good.
Scals have winked the hub caps
from his *Bovril* eyes, scratched
the paintwork of his snitch.
Spannered the Jack of his nose.
Collapsed the sub-frame of his brow.

The skin on his face stretches
like an overfilled bin-bag,
the nose pushing and shaping
like a carton protuberance.

His ears are stuck on pitta bread
with the texture of ginger nuts,
below the squashed rabbit of his hair,
above the squashed hedgehog of his beard,
around his towel rail lips
exsputory and in need of repair
like the splits in the upholstery.

Armitage Shanks

Swimming like a fish
across the avenue of carpet
the beer has gone
straight to my feet

and I step only
in the garlands in the paisley
in the carpet

and I can't hear
the paint dry, or hear
the cold inch in,

and I think
about two things
while reading graffiti
and pissing,

the joke about farting
in a space suit,
when the astronaut

clatters in.

He's stationed at the urinal.
I wait to see him
undo a few zips,

get his knob out.
But he just stands
hands on hip,

anchored, the centre-half
whose team have just
put in their own net.

My brain is made of sunshine
and the petals of flowers

the tosser who hates Manu
hammers open the door,
'Fuck off,' whispers
his carapace of vitriol.

I fuck off, everything
warns me to halt,
the door, the table,
the swirls in the carpet
urge me, stop.

Stop, go back,
stop go back. Stop. Go back,
it's only my mettle-less legs

won't listen to the sound
of knife stabbing helmet,
knife gouging space suit,

boot flying in,
spaceman inarching.

I do prefer the astronaut
to those French students
who overstepped the mark,

England V France, by being.
They did and didn't ask
it to be squared up
with a good jibbing,
cheering when France scored.
It always makes me sick

when someone smashes a glass
to swipe a throat
and I know what to do
but don't do it,
which is the opposite of
Sarathaya, the Indian entered
in the *Guinness Book Of Records,*

for among other things,
keeping his eyes open for four days
without blinking, walking backwards
for fifteen days without stopping,

He holds the records
knows what he did, but can't explain
why he did it.

Betwixt Joke and Hell

Oil and water don't mix Tolstoy.
Scrape that frog piss stinking
cuckoo nest off your daitless,
dim-witted, cod-mouthed chin.
You and me we're through boy.
I'm sick of you skid-marking
our bog, lose yourself granddad
before you feel the taste
of my fist in your Russian mush
and you can take that horse
back to Scunthorpe or Selby
or Gilberdyke or where-ever.
Shag off, eh don't get clever
or I'll knock your silly head
right into middle of next week.
Eh, eh what was that? Piss off,
go on, come on, come on then,
if you think you're hard enough.

Part Three: Verisimilitude

EXCLUSIVE POEM!
Craig Ruined My Sex Life!

It's no good. My libido dries
faster than Ghandi's flip-flop,
something withers and shrivels.
It curdles me, crosses my legs,
a repugnance to all things Liverpudlian,
The Las, Space, Thomas The Tank Engine.

I've taken folded up tissue paper
to swipe specks off the porcelain lip,
after hurling the contents of my stomach
around the bowl of the toilet.
This nausea induced by 2 Scousers
walking in the other direction,
on the other side of the street, rapping
and I'm already choosing 2 cookies
or 3, to go with milky *Horlicks?*
On the sofa in front of the box,
I'll fall asleep in a night-gown
that dresses my ankles. The love rat
upstairs, snores his ugly head off.
The bedroom's become a lonely place.
You know, in *River Island,* I came over
all queezy. I required assistance,
but the assistants can't help me.
They watched T.V. They wanted Craig
in a sex romp with me. Jesus don't remind
me of Craig, no don't, it's not funny.

Half An Igloo

Don't tickle it. Punch it laddie.
He shows me how to punch it.
Bastard. I pretend it's him,
my shirt cling-filmed to my back.
By these red industrial gloves,
my wrists all kibed and chafed,
I pack and box the snow
into the wooden snow-brick mould.

I am occupied as a builder
of igloos. I have a schedule
as tight as a huskies snatch.
So I put my sweaty back into it.
I love it. It feels euphoric
raising the most fantastic
igloo you ever clapped eyes on.

Eskimo boss has stopped bawling.
His skidoo has droned
into the frail white distance.
He doesn't want problems.
He only wants answers.
His deadline allows
no consideration for penguins
under my iced wet socks
and this polar bear is really
starting to gnaw my nipples.
For every snow-brick square I set,
while I hunker to the spirit level,
he sets too with his smudge of nose.
Each brick I lay, nudges one free
in a nonchalant game. They splatter
and break, I might laugh, kersplat,
ramshackle penguins under my boots,

but it's not his pay getting docked,
not his paws chilblaining up
and the snow smoothing my collar
melts against the nape of my neck
and it melts in the steam of my breath
and it melts in the cloud of his breath
but it takes to his fur and spreads.

Wishing Tree

There isn't a coin in the pocket
of my jeans, to peel from my palm,
not a dream that can breed for us.
A scant mention in the guidebook,
twelve miles from the nearest fencepost,
The Wishing Tree, trophying currency
jewellery, French, German, Dutch
denominations and monarchs, sovereigns,
farthings, francs, rands, brass razoos,
a language I can't quite fathom.

Ribbons of coins inlaid like buttons,
dripping off the bark like green fish-scales.
Each coin troving the weight of ambition,
bent and bashed into every crevice
and each nook with a rock, now clasped in a mantle,
each hope and dream and wish time-sealed,
as if the tree is keeping a secret,
party only to the fist of it's stash
and those that made the pilgrimage.

Those coins that spot the ground incubate
a smell of ghosts. Are those dreams lost
like drowned stars in the sea?
Here a branch in the outlying grass
nailed with a congregation of coins.
I lift it as a priest to show my wife.
To steal it would be to loot the dead.
I replace it in its exact definition.
Something pitches up of its battery,
a spirit charge of pagan religion.

Shaggy Dog Story

for Geoff Hattersley.

A man goes into a bar
and there's a duck with his bill
nailed to the floor.

False start.
A fella walks into a pub
dressed as a gorilla, landlord says,
*"Why have you got a telephone box
under your arm?"*

The man can't hear
over the volume of the donkey
in the yards relentless hee haw.

He spots a tubby jar
rammed with five pond notes,
by the bar-stooled horse,
chips in, *"Why the long face mate?"*

Backspace.
A geezer strolls into this boozer,
barman goes, "Not you again."

This guy gets visibly upset,
keeps putting his watch to his ear,
shaking it.

A nun in the corner hoots
at the inventiveness of her cure
for mother superiors constipation.

Might I mention, at this point,
the lack of anyone in the joke
having shagged the landlords missus.

Pause, fast forward.
The whole pub yawns,
it's going to be, *The Magic Parrot Story,*
when a shabby piece of string sidles in.

The landlord's missus
unleashes the killer line,
"What's time to a pig?

The piece of string shrugs his shoulders.

Mark E Smiths Cousin In a Waiting Room At A Station, Eavesdropping On Two Chinese Girls Who Might Be Japanese

Not understanding
a word they are saying,
by their giggly chatter,
I can just tell
that in the their language
they are not saying
absolutely anything
at all worth saying.

Penumbra

Or wiping glass surfaces with damp newspaper
then dusting old trophies and settling down
china cups to some sense of arrangement
and putting the cabinet door too and switching
                       the wireless on
to stop anything that might shift or unfold
out of the day, maybe Tuesday or Friday
                    or curving an ear
with the suggestion of the mantid's sole ear
centred on his chest, no sense of direction
or perception of depth,
             so Albert is skewing his head,
'*Wolverhamton Wanderers rule OK,*'
on the thumbs up emblem, poorly stitched
to his orange and black scarf.
Often accosted in the *Corner House,*
'*Name rank and number Albert,*'
bashes the heels of his boots together,
rattles it out, all shipshape and Bristol fashion,
confirming the poverty of a military order,
                a fragile shuck.
Or for ballast, for purchase, on the tarmac,
on the pavement, on the planet, his badger-legged gait
and empurpled countenance lighthousing *Cromer Street*
curb corner thrusting and parrying his stick waggling
and winking to shake off the gumption of sellotape
                     ribbon,
nattering to his own skibble head,
then there's his turkey-snatch mouth
clattering and clouting passers by
           ricocheting off cars.

Diminished Responsibility
After Derek Mahon

Or discover a spider's hideaway corner,
the idea of a cobweb teasing itself out.
Landlubbered, a ship hull submerged,
in the slow movement of a beach-sand clock.
A barnacle stuck a whole lifetime
advertising the durability of the ocean.
North-East dockyards the wind yanks window-
frames, clatters an un-listened to tantrum.
Plastic shrink-wrap ribbons tug their pallet
to seagull corners of a cemetery sky.

In the acid bath of an abandoned warehouse,
in the well of a pile of worn out tyres,
the welding gloved spectre of a once-employed hand.
Score upon score of tea cup and saucer
stacked to an estate car hatchback back-door.
This is the motor of their singular industry,
their failed car-boot sale opportunity.
Who can only find them, but insects?
Padlocked beyond the disinterest of burglary,
only nettle garlands headbutt the wind,

Lure hungry snails into their stinging midst.
They have been mopping up spider-sweat,
with spider-silk clothes lines since Dunkirk
or before, a back-seep of sand into boot-prints.
Albert compassing as a counted out boxer,
retraces a war, bomb lanced skies re-explode
on his eyelids each day. To relieve the symptoms
spooning a dose of name rank and number, heels
clapped smartly. Saluting the scrutiny of his inferiors
Private Albert destroyed to a mote,
                              mid air.

People died, and if the rust is traced
it crumbles beneath the gentlest finger.
In the hallway of a council flat leans a spade,
to slice barren un-giving allotments,
sprouting only caterpillar ridden cabbages.
Six blackened fingers trophy his days.
His volcanic angers slow eruption,
desert throated, "Move, can you move?"
His sanity nourished by catcalling
mongie, menky, spastic, flid.

On his bed a runkled pillow, an incendiary head.
Early November late October bangers, fireworks
flower a dreadlock explosion, explosion orange,
chemical green streaks of spiders legs,
extinguished but for the tail of a screamer
tagged by an odour of carbon and sulphur, bomb-sound
enough to burst an eardrum, or un-stabilise,
'Can you move, can you move?'

Collywobbler

Albert tent-pegged to this world
by his straight-legged trousers
and his Elvis Presley bendy legs.
The thigh trembling uncontrollable,
we weren't to know. Even so
it was comic to us, then
we used to do impressions of him,
un-knowing that he mightn't wobble
his petrified limbs through choice,
but now I don't know if it really is
or was comic

and it's only after all this time
that it occurs to me.

Seeing Things

You're tilted over the basin,
with a miniature plastic phial
like a doll-time hot water bottle,
a dose of *Topical Opthalmic Solution,*
the nub of your finger softly prodding
the millimetre of air in front of your eye,
air-fishing for your contact lens,
fourth or fifth dab, with a wince
and a scrape of the eyeball, landed,
it sits on the tip of your finger
like a skull cap, a carp scale,
then it's slipped into place
in it's lens holder, clipped shut
like a fob watch, then stuck
into a tub about the size of a tub
for a film of a 35mm camera,
but it's clear not black
and topped with a squirt
of contact lens solution,
left to soak till the morning.
You tip your head back like a penguin
and with a pipette technique
from the doll time bottle,
drop three drips on your cornea,
then tug your eyelids shut.
Liquid swims out at the rims.
You'd be looking at the ceiling
if your eyes weren't battened down,
like at school when the teacher
tells you to shut your eyes tightly,
or if you played hide and seek
and your counting to thirty.
I'm sitting on my hands
waiting to brush my teeth

and I've never told you this
but if you could unscrew eyeballs
like light-bulbs, I'd let you swap.

I Fall Asleep Just So You Can Wake Me Up

It must have cost her a fortune.
I've no idea where she got it.
Best Christmas present I ever had,
it was. A miniature Natalie Imbruglia,
ten inches high, not a toy or anything,
a real living little Natalie person.
I engineered a hammock for her,
by my bedside, fed her *Vegemite*
in a *Smarties* top and salted crisps.
She sings to me. Isn't that wonderful?
She's my alarm clock. She wakes me.
She jumps on my pillow, puts her hands
so tiny, to my ear and in sweet Australian
eases me out of my dreamy slumber,
"Wakey waky Petey, morning time,
come on handsome, wakey wakey Petey."

Me, and Natalie Imbruglia Taking A Swim.

Isn't she gorgeous.
But don't tell my wife.
I don't think she expected
to find me in the bath
with my little Natalie
and Natalie all naked
swimming around my knees.

The Transvestites Of Hull

If it's an automatic she
spoken without thinking,
they're at their most convincing.

Dressing-table detail more
than thought and thought through,
less bruise in the voice,

the blend in the make-up
telling of hours thumbing colour charts
and crying over blemishes,

The trim of the fringe meticulous
to the point their fastidiousness
leaves me erring over questions

Of address, Mr, Mrs, Miss, Ms.
I bet that ones not in *Debrett's*.

A long skirt can streamline slopes
reserved for blokes, the ham-shank calves
a dead giveaway, or a masculine gait,

or the shape of the face,
but there's no hoodwinking anyone
if they haven't shaved,

rasp like Les Dawson,
in an implausible hairpiece
mismatched and skewiff,

fidgeting with the straps
of their over the shoulder turnip holder.
I don't want to break their spell,

this magic trick that they are
women, but you can only notice
when they open out their hands,

their massive wanking hands,
built for picking potatoes,
building ships or laying bricks.

Could a surgeon give them
nimble fingers? Did I tell you
about sexy legs Norman?

He knows how to wear high-heels
and even though he's a bloke
he's got a nice pins and a lovely arse.

He could fuss and dither all day
over a dainty matching handbag
for his slenderest white skirt.

How you can't see his bollocks
hanging out, I've no idea,
and what of his bollocks?

Tolstoy's Fried Egg

Donald Duck spitting and drowning,
the sound of a hot egg frying.
His egg yolk, egg yolk yellow,
egg white not yet fried egg white.

Rusty bacon wraps the air in bacon,
the gas on five, rind just crisp,
fat still hot, switch the switch off.
Bread-knife resting on the breadboard,

under the grill, cut bread, turned off.
Eggshell halves cupped on the right,
teabag nestling dry as tinder
in the bottom of a united mug.

The cold smooth plastic of the milk-
carton sits snug in the door in the fridge,
a splodge of milk the size of a small coin
yet to drop on the formica top.

Crunchy nut cornflakes wait in the box,
the bowl in the cupboard, the spoon
in the drawer, Annabel's key in the lock
in the door, of Tolstoy neither hide nor hair.

It's all so quiet and weird, I can hear
the footsteps of a fly on the wall.
The kettle is un-poured, yet recently boiled,
barely hot to scald or brew a weak cup of tea.

Biographies and
Acknowledgements

Jo Pearson

Born into a one time mining family in Ossett, West Yorkshire in 1970, Jo Pearson was brought up on Merseyside, returning in 1984 with a scouse accent at the height of the miner's strike. Jo studied music and psychology in York and London and worked in Edinburgh as a music therapist. She is now eurythmy pianist at York Steiner School. Jo began writing prose poetry in the mid 1990's. Not a performer, Jo prefers to let her poems speak from the page. Published widely in the small presses, this is Jo's first full collection. Talking to the Virgin Mary explores legacy and its effect on the individual and the social, identity and its expression through appearance and perception and communication, the wafer thin mint dividing sanity and reality.

Acknoweldgements

The author would like to thank the following presses where her poems were first published: *Still Born: Orbis International* No. 111, 1998; *Fatalism; Skald,* Bangor University, No. 8, 1998; *Message to a Friend: The Reater,* Wrecking Ball Press, No. 2. 1998; *Taxi Man: Terrible Work,* No. 9, 1999; *Trolleys around the World: ENVOI,* No.122, 1999; *Someone's New Home and An Unplayed Piano Grimaces* (versions): *Opening Line Magazine,* Yorkshire Arts Circus, No. 2, 1999.

Thanks to:

The author would like to thank the following people for their support and inspiration: Chris, Matt, Al, Brian, Rico, Peter, Dandelion, Steve and everyone at route and on the Opening Line.

Daithidh MacEochaidh

Mad Mac's poetry is informed by the absurdity of the mundane, the injustice of the quotidian boot in the face, and the senselessness of drawing the next breath. Despite sticking the flip-flop into a fully formalised nihilism, his poems rage against the tame, banal niceties of poetic craft in favour of the scansion of the head-butt, the iambic explosion of a Tourettic F.U. and a manic metric syntax charged with semtex. All this laced with poisonous wit, humour and the smile of the successful suicide.

Thanks

A big thank you to all the bari gajes, khusty charvas and ald mukkers at route for collecting this — most folk would be collecting up the poems here with a poopa-scoopa and a big pair of plastic gloves — God bless 'em. Joe Patterson and the Amble Writers Group deserve a big pat on the back, as certain poems were knocked up, down or about whilst attending that fine establishment and under the patient and lang suffering tutelage of Joe — good God, they don't pay the man, half-ways enough. Yet, the most gratitude is due to all the mad feckers, including masel', who have had a big part in creating the facts behind many of these poems; and ah'm reet sorry that I can't print the real stories, as nay one has a willing suspension of disbelief willing enough to sustain belief enough for a read like that. As for false belief as a premise in a true conclusion see Bertrand Russell. Enough said, sithee anon.

Peter Knaggs

Peter Knaggs is interested in how the ordinary and extraordinary interweave. His poetry is about storytelling and characters. Informed by modern poetics and culture, Cilla Black has as much to do with the outcome as Simic, O'Brien, Sweeney or Armitage. *Tolstoy On A Horse,* is a chronicle of his time spent as poet in residence of his own home, 75 Chanterlands Avenue, Hull.

Thanks

The author would like to thank Rhodesy, Suthers, Birdsy, Daley & Smith, Claffo, and Sean Body of The Reater, Dreamcatcher, Rue Bella, Route Newspaper, Poetry Last Thursday, Brando's Hat and the editors of Whang, and The Slouch for unleashing some of these poems on to an unsuspecting public.

A Woman On Chanterlands Avenue Peels a Potato And *Guy Fawkes* featured in the New Forest Poetry Society, Competition Anthology 2000.

Other Titles From Route -Fiction

Like A Dog To Its Vomit
Daithidh MacEochaidh
ISBN: 1 901927 07 5 £6.95
Somewhere between the text, the intertext and the testosterone find Ron Smith, illiterate book lover, philosopher of non-thought and the head honcho's left-arm man. Watch Ron as he oversees the begging franchise on Gunnarsgate, shares a room with a mouse of the Lacota Sioux and makes love to Tracy back from the dead and still eager to get into his dungarees. There's a virgin giving birth under the stairs, putsch at the taxi rank and Kali, Goddess of Death, is calling. Only Arturo can sort it, but Arturo is travelling. In part two find out how to live in a sock and select sweets from a shop that time forgot and meet a no-holds barred state registered girlfriend. In part three, an author promises truth, but the author is dead - isn't she?

In this complex, stylish and downright dirty novel, Daithidh MacEochaidh belts through underclass underachieving, postponed-modern sacrilege and the more pungent bodily orifices.

Very Acme
Adrian Wilson
ISBN: 1 901927 12 1 £6.95
New Nomad, nappy expert, small town man and ultimately a hologram – these are the life roles of Adrian Wilson, hero and author of this book, which when he began writing it, was to become the world's first novel about two and a half streets. He figured that all you ever needed to know could be discovered within a square mile of his room, an easy claim to make by a man who's family hadn't moved an inch in nearly seven centuries.

All this changes when a new job sends him all around the world, stories of Slaughter and the Dogs and Acme Terrace give way to Procter and Gamble and the Russian Mafia. He starts feeling nostalgic for the beginning of the book before he gets to the end.

Very Acme is two books within one, it is about small town life in the global age and trying to keep a sense of identity in a world of multi-corporations and information overload.

Crazy Horse
Susan Everett
ISBN 1 901927 06 7 £6.95
Jenny Barker, like many young women, has a few problems. She is trying to get on with her life, but it isn't easy. She was once buried underneath the sand and it had stopped her growing up, plus she had killed the milkman. Her beloved horse has been stolen while the vicious *Savager* is on the loose cutting up animals in fields. She's neither doing well in college nor in love and fears she may die a virgin.

Crazy Horse is a wacky ride.

Other Titles From Route -Poetry

I Am
Michelle Scally-Clarke
ISBN 1 901927 08 3 £10 Including free CD
At thirty years old, Michelle is the same age as the mother who gave her up
into care as a baby. In the quest to find her birth parents, her roots and her own
identity, this book traces the journey from care, to adoption, to motherhood, to
performer. Using the fragments of her own memory, her poetry and extracts
from her adoption files, Michelle rebuilds the picture of 'self' that allows her
to transcend adversity and move forward to become the woman she was born
to be.
You can hear the beat and song of Michelle Scally-Clarke on the CD that
accompanies this book and, on the inside pages, read the story that is the
source of that song.

Moveable Type
Rommi Smith
ISBN 1 901927 11 3 £10 Including free CD
It is the theme of discovery that is at the heart of *Moveable Type*. Rommi Smith
takes the reader on a journey through identity, language and memory, via
England and America, with sharp observation, wit and wry comment en 'route.
The insights and revelations invite us not only to look beneath the surface of
the places we live in, but also ourselves.
Moveable Type and its accompanying CD offer the reader the opportunity to
listen or read, read and listen. Either way, you are witnessing a sound that is
uniquely Rommi Smith.

All titles available from good bookshops and can be purchased online at
www.route-online.com
or direct from the route office
tel 01977 603028